COUPLE'S JOURNEY

Restore, Relearn, Rejoice

Rey Abarca & Annie Abarca

Printed in the United States of America

ISBN: 9798303219243

10 9 8 7 6 5 4 3 2 1

EMPIRE PUBLISHING
www.empirebookpublishing.com

Cover Photo by
www.dantemarcelo.com?

For our children
Franchesca, Theron and Kira

Contents

INTRODUCTION

Many of us desire a good marriage and it will indeed be a blessing to be married to someone willing to pursue a similar or very related passion in this life. Such a nice desire and indeed very noble. Yet we can't ignore the reality that marriage is challenged by so many factors in today's culture and difficult circumstances. It has become a matter of how well we can stand in firmness against all these odds. What surprises us are the numbers that undeniably define the hunger to build a strong marriage, despite having a good amount of reliable resources of support available today. As per the latest statistics and rates studies from the CDC and Pew Research Centers;

- The USA has a 2.4 divorce rate per 1000 total population for the year 2022. It's an improved rate compared to 4.0 in 2000 but the 2.4 rate is still considered a high rate compared to other countries (excludes data from California, Hawaii, Indiana, Minnesota, and New Mexico)[1]

- As per the PEW Research Center, out of a sample of 4752 individuals, the divorce rate for Protestants (identified as non-Catholic Christians) was approximately 51%, and it is the highest among other religious groups [2]

---

[1] CDC. National Center for Health Statistics.(March 13, 2024) Marriage and Divorce. www.cdc.gov

[2] PEW Research Center. (June 13, 2022). Religion in America: U.S. Religious Data Demographics and Statistics. Pew Research Center's Religion & Public life Project. www.pewresearch.org

We could have fallen on those rates when we faced a very challenging situation that shook our marriage and family relationships. We're thankful that God intervened and saved us from any future damages we could have taken, which will hardly impact our three children. Since then, our life journey has changed, but along the way, we've collected a lot of learnings and genuine realizations. Like the surprising discoveries of how our past life circumstances and established behaviors significantly impacted our marriage. As well as understanding the authenticity of Christian living, and the continuous redemptive journey with Jesus Christ.

Despite today's blessings of available resources and easy access to information, we realize that there's still a high need for restoration, relearning, and living a life that genuinely rejoices God. We're not your typical literature experts backed up with strong theological education. We're regular individuals who experienced real-life challenges and our willingness to share this story is to show that Jesus Christ is alive and transforming people. Since it's a co-authored book, you will see a lot of pronouns;

- I (name) - means that a particular portion is shared by such a person
- We (Rey & Annie) - means we're putting emphasize that a particular story is our experience and may not apply to others
- We, Us - welcomes readers who find great similarities in such experiences

May our collected testimonies, and acquired learnings from gifted speakers, teachers, and authors that are parallel in Biblical truths may serve an encouragement to any individual or married couple. May the shared truths speak strongly that you could also take that step in making bold changes, and together let's continue collecting testimonies that Jesus Christ is alive and transforming lives and marriages.

"Welcome to the **'Couple's Journey.'**"

CHAPTER 1
GENUINE REALIZATION

The biggest blockage for a genuine realization is our self. It's the most difficult reality to face and the most challenging to overcome.

We lived this life with perspectives and beliefs that we collected over time. We think they are good enough to equip us to move forward in this so-called life. We learned to set specific standards that helped us to navigate this life and rested on the idea of validity by results that are acceptable in our surroundings or culture. Hoping those results could provide freedom, security, and comfort. Thus, it becomes an ultimate goal in living this life. Those objectives and intents are pleasing and acceptable. They are noble, but disconnection starts to sink in when we try to focus on those rather than being anchored to the One who gifted this life to us.

Similarly, in our relationship as husband and wife, we look forward to having someone who can give us freedom within the sanctity of marriage, security, and comfort. [Pic 1 - Rey & Annie's Wedding] Although our love story is not the usual story of two single individuals falling in love with each other, and easily adapted to married life just like many. We both have our stakes in our previous relationships. One has been divorced twice, and the other one has managed not to sign a "document" but has been in many relationships. We both got tired of all the pain and challenges of our own experiences and almost gave up on having that "someone."

4

When we were just about to lose hope completely, circumstances changed, and we got that opportunity to meet. This time, things seem to be turning in a better direction. Maybe because we've learned so much and become more aware of the various factors of this so-called "relationship." We both knew what we wanted, and we agreed on how to reach our goal - to have our own family.

We managed to gain confidence in each other and the relationship we're trying to build. Such enthusiasm was solidified with learnings from previous relationships and clear family goals. We tried to look at every facet, and we're checking each box with great hope. Not knowing that there's more sitting in the core of each of our hearts. The

5

pain and confusion collected since we became aware of our existence in this world. We lost the thought of knowing that our perspective of the marital relationship and family concept was deeply impacted by our experiences from our own family. As well as those we've seen in the surroundings that, by the looks, seem to be working out fine and happy.

The unaddressed pain and unclear confusion took a deep space in our hearts. Such space becomes numb over time as we survive and endure this life. Not knowing that it will float as we go deeper into our marital relationship. As challenges become more complicated and we're losing comprehension to somehow make things sensible, the pain that's been hiding in our hearts starts to levitate. The portion of our hearts that's been numb for quite a while suddenly becomes more sensitive, especially as we witness the pain and suffering that is now being passed on to our children. Suddenly, the complete numbness is no longer effective. Our hearts felt more profound pain, and the perspective that once provided confidence and hope was suddenly shaken. We're seeing our hands losing control of what has given us freedom, security, and comfort. We're losing each other. We're losing hope.

It was a little over a month after Rey and I (Annie) received SBA- Nevada recognition as a minority-owned small business of the year- in 2018 when the business started to go south. [Pic 2 - SBA Award] It could have been something that would provide such a level of confidence, considering that we are an immigrant couple who has experienced wonderful opportunities in this country that we called a "second home." Yet the enthusiasm just sat in for a very short period and was immediately replaced with deep concerns and heavy pressure like a tightrope that drove me to move forward.

Abarca's children holding Rey and Annie's trophy and poster recognition as the 2018 SBA-Nevada Minority-Owned Small Business

In that early morning drive to our warehouse, my first episode of realization sank in! I may have "some " that could have been already "good," but my heart and mind are insensate for genuine peace and happiness. I vividly remember myself as a young girl and actively living between home, school, and church. I didn't have that much then, but I was living with sincere joy and peace with God.

7

Quickly, I realized, where's God in my life now?! We may not have much compared to others with similar life statuses, but I have more than I used to have. So, I took a quick moment to speak with God while the red light was on. It was a simple prayer which I didn't expect God to act immediately. I still remember the words that felt like a strong plea, "O God, save me. I'm living a life with no peace and true happiness. I want to go back to that state where I have You. I want to have genuine peace and sincere happiness. In Jesus' name, Amen" As the green light allowed me to pass through the intersection, I felt tears on both cheeks. That prayer was indeed a quick reminder and act to call for help. As soon as I arrived in my office, I went on as usual in my routine.

As the weeks passed, we noticed changes in the business. Rey tried to get my (Annie's) attention, but my response didn't take his words seriously. My confidence in the 'little achievement' we received has put a sense of uncertainty in my mind and heart that things will be fine. It's just a season! But the season turns to more weeks of challenges. One night, I found myself searching the net for a business resolution. It was past 1:00 AM, and the perseverance started to weigh down. My frustration didn't just define the unsuccessful search for business resolution but also the hard impact on our family - in my relationship with my husband. It was not too long ago that we celebrated the business achievement, and now we are close to calling it quits. The only thing that holds us together is our children. In that very dark home office, where lights are only coming from my computer monitor, I had a quick flashback on how I witnessed my own parents' disagreements in finances. I felt heartbroken when the day came that my father just quickly packed his clothes and left. Am I repeating it? Will I allow this business turmoil to deeply put pain in our relationship that we'll lose each other? I need help. We need help.

I (Annie) quickly changed the keywords in the search engine and looked for a spiritual support group that I could join. I need to go back to the One who I knew would provide comfort, guidance, and help. I must return to the One who provides genuine peace and sincere happiness. I must return to the One who will guide and help me escape this messy situation and return to a peaceful relationship with my husband. I must go back to God.

The hard days continued to move forward, and I (Rey) noticed Annie slowly incorporating God into our family. While she's starting to turn to God for our situation, I continue to rationalize things and make them logical. However, I noticed our obvious condition but I didn't give that much attention to how heavily Annie was affected and my responses to our circumstances have added fear and loneliness to her. The business problem was making a significant impact on her. While I have a straightforward and structured perspective of all the circumstances. The business was her idea and her initial effort to get it running. I only jumped into it when I found myself challenged in securing a new job after retiring from the twenty (20) years of military service in the US Navy. I'm not fully attracted to the nature of the business, but after some time, my liking for it changed. I noticed the income it brings to our family and the opportunities to help others when we started hiring employees. When I foresaw a potential hard financial impact that the business was about to face, I tried to explain it to Annie. My effort to get her attention was not enough to distract her. She had full confidence and faith in the business operations that she built and established. So when the crisis officially impacted the business and our family, my mind was set on the idea that it was all her fault. I reached the point of not giving much effort, so I decided to stay within my day-to-day routine and attend to my usual responsibilities. Yet, the moments of expressing my frustrations and anger towards the situation had become more frequent.

Difficulties in life are not unusual for me. I (Rey) grew up in a broken family. At a very young age, I witnessed the painful challenges that my father brought to our family, and I've seen how it impacted my mother. At the same time, I have my own painful experiences in the abusive hands of my father. As I continue to collect learnings and experiences, I'm also harboring pain and anger that eventually leads to toughness in my heart. I've learned to survive and endure difficulties in this life, but it molded me with deep anger and grudges. I didn't realize the load of anger in my heart until I saw the impact of my responses to the challenges that Annie and I had to go through. I'm a man of few words, but my expression of disappointment is very evident. Temper has become my protection. So, no more pain will go further in my heart, which is already heavily covered by my unpleasant experiences since childhood.

As I (Rey) witnessed Annie go through pain and fear, I was just within my "zone," waiting for her next move. My mind was already set on where these circumstances will lead us. Not realizing that staying in that "zone," I let my wife feel alone in the battle, and insecurities in the relationship started to build up in her heart and mind. My little confidence in going through this challenging season was not in a solid partnership between me and Annie. I've

10

survived before, so I know I will have it again this time. I didn't care how it impacted her as long as we remained civil in the partnership that we're having for the sake of our three children. It was a very unhealthy and heavy perspective to live with during that time. It took me a lot to notice the reality that I was in my third marriage, but I was still living "alone."

Realization may seem easy. We can easily enumerate instances in our lives where we quickly nod on things and have such realization. Yet, "genuine realization" is different. It's a complete acceptance of shortcomings that will drive you into repentance thus leading to actions desiring for genuine transformation. It's a process of brokenness, restored in humility, resulting in genuine transformation. It's like a layer of "surrendering" is being peeled off. Or surrendering a wall of "self-protection" that we've been holding onto to manage our endurance as we move forward. The incomplete deliverance of past pains and challenges somehow left layers or walls of protection in our hearts. A defense that we thought would be good enough so future pains and challenges would not have the same hard impact as what we used to experience. A cover that will stand firm in discouragement and let us hold on for a quick recovery enough to move forward. Sounds pretty good, but what will happen when circumstances break down those layers or walls of "self-protection"? When it's tough to pick up the pieces and be able to restore for a quick patch of recovery. How are we going to respond? How are we going to move forward?

We had our initial hard blow that requires genuine realization. It was challenging and caught us by surprise. The responses we used to do that let us go through previous circumstances are no longer working. Our first picture for genuine realization is accepting that we need to undergo a process of brokenness in these unhealthy habits and wrong perspectives. There are more on our list, but we're sharing these five (5) in which we find ourselves challenged big time in that initial blow for genuine realization. This encouraged us to change gears and have significant changes in our relationship.

1. Rationalizing Things

Rationalization is the most common, and subtle, and could result in a dangerous behavior. As most defined, rationalization is an attempt to explain or justify with logical, plausible reasons, even if these are not true or appropriate. Naturally, rationalizing is a way of making excuses. It is so common and subtle that we become so comfortable with it. The dangerous part is experiencing the big blow of consequences after a certain period. The "first couple" illustrated the process and results of rationalization. Adam said, "The woman whom You gave to be with me, she gave me from the tree, and I ate." (Genesis 3:12b, NASB1995). Then Eve responded, "The serpent deceived me, and I ate." (Genesis 3:13b, NASB1995). The words expressed by Adam and Eve defined their effort to rationalize the sin that they had committed when asked by the Lord.

Sadly, in our relationship, it's becoming a normal behavior for us to extract any available resources and comprehension that will justify the situation, our perspectives, our actions, and our chosen resolution. The more time we spend on this justification, the more opportunities we'll waste for more impactful solutions. It's a very exhausting response because reasoning without a solid reference foundation will surely be an endless justification. In every marital conflict we had, we spent so much time rationalizing without knowing that it was already causing more pain, more confusion, and a clear path leading to potential destruction. Every conflict and argument we had is circulated in rationalizing things. Whenever we need to decide, we rely solely on our logical justification. We didn't notice how our hearts and minds were utterly dimmed with rationalization. Until at that sudden moment, we caught ourselves creating logical and valid explanations to justify our obvious sinful behavior. Our intellectual reasoning based on the knowledge accumulated from our past experiences and selfish desires is leading us to spiritual escapism. We saw a clear direction directing us to complete destruction.

It's a bad habit developed with a poor foundation of selfish desire and foolishness. We must commit ourselves to breaking this bad habit and replacing it with something that will lead us to selfless love and healthy perspectives. If we don't, we'll move forward, always rationalizing things, whether in conflict or making decisions. Don't let it reach the day when rationalization makes you impotent and unable to take effective action. We struggle to accept that we're enslaved by this behavior, and it's not an easy road to complete deliverance. As we're writing this book, we have to admit that there are still instances when we're tempted to fall into the pitfalls of rationalization and making excuses. It's a consistent process of faithfully and joyfully reassuring ourselves about our relationship and identity in Jesus Christ.

It's only by the grace of God that we're able to establish a spiritual habit of anchoring our lives in God's words. Our breakfast has become a sharing session on how we, individually, encountered God on that day. It's not always a light discussion and sometimes triggers the difference in our personalities, but doing this habit over time has opened our eyes to the unified messages God wants to bring to our attention. You'll learn more about our experience in Chapter 6 when God enlightened us with His unified and directly related messages. The difficulties in overcoming rationalization constantly drive us to rely on God's grace and love.

II. Cuddling Self-Pity

Another typical and subtle unpleasant behavior. The scariest is that we're living in a generation that is normalizing and making it acceptable. When someone tries to put a light on this dangerous behavior, it's an automatic conclusion of not being compassionate or loving. Nowadays, we also have more prominent platforms in trying to embrace this behavior such as social media, ads, campaigns, movies, and other public sources who aim for massive influence.

As we awkwardly recognized the unhealthy effect of this behavior, we realized how we're so consumed with self-pity in every disagreement, fight, and uncomfortable situation. We've been crafty about it; indeed, the husband and wife have different ways of practicing it. Even when we only want to be with friends and help us process what we're going through, we end our dialogue in a self-pity tone. Next thing you know, two camps are forming - one for the husband and one for the wife. There's this desire that others will feel our woundedness and admire us for being "mistreated ." It's easy to succumb to self-pity, particularly in a marital relationship. One minute, we're this loving and sacrificing individual in this relationship; the next minute, we're hurt and bitter that all our dedication, sacrifices, and hard work are not being noticed or appreciated. We used the weapon of "self-pity" to indulge gratification on our selfish appetites. There's this one day, as we continue to press on with this war of "self-pity," we miss counting the days of not communicating properly inside the house. We survived passing the days by attending to our usual routine. Then, the day became hectic, and we assumed the other would pick up the children in school. Then we received a call from the school that our children were the only ones waiting for pick-up. It's such a shame to witness the effect on our children.

There are no positive accomplishments in self-pity. It's simply a great excuse for our unwillingness to take responsibility for the situation and our responses in a certain period. If we're not guarding our hearts properly, the delay we're adding is just a silent war of self-pity. This behavior is putting us more in the problem of "sight." Our vision is mainly focused on ourselves and the circumstances that we're dealing with. Rather than crying out for help and guidance to God for whatever level of distress we have, self-pity will enslave us in the misery of our hearts. The more we ignore and unwillingly experience God's attributes, the more we're soaking ourselves into a potential deep hole of self-pity. This leads us to carry all the burden, rely on ourselves, and take comfort in cuddling with self-pity. We can win over falling into the temptation of this unpleasant behavior as we continue to learn, embrace, and live a life relying on God's grace and sovereignty. It's not a quick fix and surely requires a process. He is the ultimate authority in our lives; He will not allow certain things to pass on far from His divine will and purpose. If we knew that we could get genuine comfort and guidance from God, our marital relationship and some crucial factors circulating in it would have been different.

III. Quickness to Blame

Funny how we know that this will not bring any form of goodness in ourselves, our relationships, and our lives, yet we still let ourselves fall into this trap and move forward as if getting away with it is impossible. Like self-pity, the "quickness to blame" is another "vision" problem. It's our often response, so the frustration will draw directly to others and avoid our contributions to the circumstances. We're too prideful to accept our participation and even take action to be contributors to solid resolutions.

"It's Dad's fault" has become a standard line inside our household. If something goes wrong or any unexpected circumstances, there's a default thinking that it's Dad's (Rey's) fault. It's so overused that it became a joke in our home. When our business problem started, our heavy "blaming game" cycle began to the point that we lost ourselves amid our critical situation. We blamed each other, our former employees, the business' sales channels, vendors, the economy, and even the government. The moment we couldn't find any more entity to blame was when we caught ourselves totally lost in the situation. Leading us to complex configurations and challenging implementation of resolutions. Another ugly consequence when we continue to play this game with our spouse is for our partner to lose their confidence and even identity in the relationship. Where it should be a safe venue for our partner for healthy expression and processing of thoughts, empowered for new opportunities and being loved, the consistent practice of blame led them to the most uncomfortable relationship.

It is unfortunate to witness our partners get lost in the relationship and unable to do their role, which is supposedly God's design. How we wish there was an easy manual that we can use to easily overcome this "quickness-to-blame" but this behavior was strongly formed and solidified over some time. Also, this behavior often relates and blends well with our effort to understand the circumstances. When we try to ask questions, dig deeper into the situation, and investigate for understanding, we're walking on eggshells to the temptation of blaming others. Our effort to let our partner take responsibility and own their actions is quickly misinterpreted as part of the "blaming" game.

Whether we're evidently playing this "blaming" game, recipient of the blame, or strongly misinterpreted due to an aggressive approach, this behavior is not easy to overcome. It requires process and intentionality to pursue breakthroughs. It's only by the grace of God that we can commit ourselves to getting out of this behavior. Annie and I (Rey) have to constantly remind ourselves that we're not enemies to play this game anymore. The real enemy (Satan) is actively pushing married couples to play this game so there will be division. We'll share more of our experience and learnings in the reality of evil today in Chapter 5. Keeping this in mind, we've established a commitment that in every incident, we're above this game, and our effort to understand the situation is for our pursuance to unitedly seek God's will, purposes, and ways. The constant reminder of the greatness of God's love through Jesus Christ and its impact on our lives, the more likely we'll yield to the power of the Holy Spirit and not fall into Satan's temptation of "blaming" games.

IV. Guarded "Comfort Zone"

Another subtle practice in marriage that's slowly becoming a standard today. It's a corrupt practice that highly impacts the oneness of two individuals in marriage. Initially, we thought we were doing good in terms of this oneness until things got more complicated, and then we realized the established "comfort zone" we built over the years. It's not just about attitude or expectations. This guarded "comfort zone" impacts some crucial factors in married life. Home management, financials, parenting strategy, and reference to the proper foundation of our relationship.

We didn't know that we created this "compartmentalized" married life where we managed to be comfortable in our respective sections and carefully guard ourselves around the boundaries. Our decisions and choices were not based on building a solid oneness foundation but on keeping our boundaries safe as we continue to survive in this married life. So, when the circumstances strongly affected our "comfortable zones," it triggered us to find resolutions that would immediately bring back the comfort we were enjoying in our respective zones. We'll discuss this further as we share our learnings of God's intended design for marriage in Chapter 3. It was a big a-ha moment for both of us, as we learned that our partnership was for "endurance" rather than joyfully living in this wonderful God's gift of relationship. It's not having a storm-free life, but rather a stormproof one. It's a couple's journey with inner peace and happiness despite challenges.

V. Ignorance About True Life

The bad behavior patterns mentioned are truly evident in our broken connection with God through Jesus Christ. We're navigating this marriage apart from Him, who's the Creator and Designer of our lives and our marriage.

When we faced that initial big challenge in our marital relationship, we realized how wrongly we'd perceived this life. Our actions and the ways we used to manage our emotions and decisions were based on a poor foundation that's hollow and slack. It was heartbreaking to witness how we were tossing pain to each other, to our children, and even to some people who were close to us. Our understanding, learnings, and standards were truly tested, and we have a clear vision of how everything started to fall apart. We're certainly on the edge, and foolishness is still denying it. We knew that we needed an overhaul for us to move forward effectively. We knew that, and we understood it, but the overwhelming pain and realization caught us in confusion. Confused about where and how to start this genuine resolution. It was at that moment that we heard God's call very clearly. This time, we need to move forward with the intention of having God in our lives, relationships, and family.

All the while, we thought we had Him in our lives. We go to church regularly. We're diligent in bringing our children to Sunday School and Summer Vacation Bible School. From time to time, we speak to Him through

19

prayers. We thought we were doing fine. Then, our realization continues that what we have is a religion - a traditional act of having God in our lives, but God should not be put in a box of "religion." His existence is not just a regular Sunday activity or summer Bible camp. He wants us to have a relationship with Him - an intimate relationship. Our connection with Him reflects how we perceive this life, leading us to how to live with it. Our lifestyle defines what kind of relationship we have with God. At that very moment, we finally got our genuine realization that we need to be intentional in anchoring our lives to God.

It's a difficult and painful journey to go through, just to have a good visual and recognition of our shortcomings. When we're making such a list of unhealthy habits and wrong perspectives, we're reminded of further complications that could have been prevented. At the same time, our great disconnection with God has let us hold on to the perspective that we can always go through circumstances and live this life with our effort and skills. We're so wrong and when we both recognized God's clear call we knew that we needed to change our course. This time, it is in pursuit of Him.

CHAPTER 2
RESPONDING TO GOD'S CALL

Just like most couples, our pursuit of God didn't come at the same time. It was Annie who started to intentionally incorporate God into our situation and eventually into our family. I (Rey) once woke up in the middle of the night catching her sitting on our bathroom floor crying out loud because of our overwhelming situation. Then it was replaced with her early morning visit in our guest room and would spend hours of prayer and reading the Bible. She'll come out with evidence of heavy crying but she's excited and hopeful. We used to exchange rundowns of our activities for the day during breakfast, but Annie started to share how she encountered God every morning. Our situation hasn't changed. She's hopeful that God will help us with our problems. While still showing deep concerns, there were moments when she was anxious. Yet, she'll bounce back quickly and her commitment to stay with God strongly speaks through her words and actions. She will pray numerous times within a day. I will see her at home praying in our guest room and I will also catch her under her office table praying to God. It became so obvious that I would make fun of her even in front of our children.

She kept me informed and aware of the online Sunday Services she's watching and her regular online small group sessions. I noticed that it was helping her but it was not enough to completely satisfy my curiosity or interest. My mind was set on the belief that I was doing my part in this spiritual aspect of life. Although I'm not religious compared

21

to many who I knew believed in the same faith, I do recognize God and His authority.

Like many families in the Philippines, I (Rey) grew up in a household practicing a famous religion in that country. I diligently visited church on Sundays, memorizing prayers and other religious traditions. I didn't see that strong connection to God in our day-to-day lives besides Sunday and other religious activities throughout the year. Even when I moved to the United States, I carried the beliefs and traditions. It wasn't difficult for me to continue doing what I usually do in the Philippines because of the available churches in the states I moved into. As well as my family and relatives are continuously practicing the same religion. I had some moments when I cried prayers to God due to my parent's separation and how it slowly made hard impacts on my life. The pain of brokenness continues to go deeper in my heart as I find myself living with relatives and not in a regular household with my parents. At a young age, I learned to live independently and build a new life in this new country with minimal supervision from my parents. With a broken connection between God's existence to my dysfunctional family, my perception of Him was just centered on not letting myself fall into any bad behavior that would disobey God's ten (10) commandments. Instead, my mind and heart were set on the idea that I just needed to move forward doing good works so these circumstances in my life would finally end. I used to equate God's blessings with comfort in life. I have to do consistent and collective good works to receive God's blessings. I let such beliefs be rooted in my mind and my heart. So, even if Annie is showing a different connection with God, I'm blinded by the thought that our circumstances will eventually change but in different ways.

On the other hand, I (Annie) started viewing our circumstances from a different perspective. Although there were moments when my deep concerns were evident. I bounced back as I was elevated with excitement to be reconnected with God. I discovered one of my favorite preachers in the Philippines through YouTube. I'm so happy to see him back in the ministry after some time. It was one of his preachings that encouraged me to be connected in an online small group. The group helped me to stay connected and consistent in spiritual discussion. My revived faith has brought me to so much hunger in God's words. I realized that I've lived many years of just being a "church-goer" despite knowing God at a young age. The small group helped me to be intentional in my faith.

Unlike Rey, I (Annie) grew up in a family exposed to Bible studies, Summer Youth Camps, and lively Sunday Services. Although I was young then, I vividly remember a group of missionaries visiting houses in our block and their efforts in sharing the Gospel. Our family is one of the households to hear about the Good News and Christianity. My mother, aunt, and grandmother responded accordingly and embraced this new truth about Jesus Christ. My childhood memories include active participation in Christian church and ministries. I was 9 years old when my mind accommodated a serious thought about heaven and hell. I was upstairs in our home, looking at the sky through our window when I first prayed to God. At that young age, a great fear of hell developed in my heart. So, I told God that I didn't want to go to hell and desire to grow in Christianity by diligently attending Sunday services. At a young age, I allowed myself to be used in the ministries or any contribution to the church operations. Since then, I had opportunities to get to know God through Summer Youth Camps and other church activities.

The church allowed me (Annie) to grow and travel to different places for camps, prayer gatherings, and even congregational fasting. Even though there was heavy resistance from my father, I continued practicing Christianity. I accepted Jesus Christ as my personal Lord and Savior at a young age. I got to know Him through church, but outside that building, Christianity was very challenging - even in our own house. I didn't expect my love for God at a very young age would result in a heavy rejection from my father.

We used to live in a very simple 2-story home. Our upstairs was just an open space enough to accommodate our shared dresser and sleeping space. One afternoon, I was alone upstairs on my knees and intensely praying. When my father caught me, he rolled a towel and threw it at me. Although it was not painful, the rolled towel was hard enough to move my head when it hit me. To my surprise, I stopped and looked at him. For that brief moment, I lost words but my eyes were asking the question, "Why?" He then simply commented, "Oh I thought you were going crazy." He left smiling. It wasn't the first time that he boldly expressed his disappointment and rejection of the faith I chose. He barely hit us maybe because he's seldom home and trying to catch up on his role as a father. Yet his words are strong enough that could heavily stab our hearts and leave a very painful mark. There were times when I was eating, he would talk constantly expressing his objection to Christianity. At first, I tried to defend my choice of faith but

24

eventually, I gave up and just took every word coming out of his heavy mouth. I can't do anything but shed tears hoping that it will encourage him to stop.

My father was in the military, stationed in Manila, away from our home in the province of Bataan. He will just be with us in a few schedules over the year. One time, when he came home and discovered my pursuit of Christianity continued. This time his objection was more aggressive. He took me and my brother to the local Cathedral church and asked the person in charge to open the door for us. When inside, he ordered me and my brother to kneel down and march on our tiny knees going to the front with all those altars. I was standing firm trying to make a stand that my knees are only for a living God. My rejection was evident but my brother told me to do it as strangers started to fill up the church. I quietly obeyed but inside I was screaming to God. I journey on those challenging days alone. I may have shared with a few people but I don't remember receiving any bold support back then. I continued to stand firm in faith and my father eventually gave in.

I've also witnessed the challenges of my parents' relationship, which stems from their two different faiths and beliefs. When I hit teenage life, and my school activities got busier, it affected my engagement in the church. I let my young self be involved in a relationship with a guy that led me to wrong choices and actions that were indeed not pleasing to God. I started to hide things, lie, and be physically intimate with the guy I was dating then. My journey in Christianity was compromised. I tried to stay in the loop by attending Sunday Services and remained in such a habit even when I married Rey.

Now that I'm (Annie) entering into a new season of my life, I'm noticing a different impact of the Gospel. It could have been influenced by my current roles as a wife, mother to three children, and entrepreneur. My desire to be anchored in Jesus Christ is far different from being an active church-goer. The regular spiritual discussion with my online small group was a good help to stay consistent in this new journey. The couple that stood as our small group leaders were patiently attending and guiding me with my questions and concerns. Despite the surprisingly good experiences with the small group, I'm still keeping certain boundaries in the group. My fear and shame of the magnitude of our problems have kept me to certain boundaries in sharing information with the group. I need help yet I'm not being honest on the decree of help I needed.

One morning as I (Annie) was attending to my usual admin work in the office, I felt a sudden pain in my chest. I immediately called Rey and he said that my sitting posture could be putting more pressure on my chest. I changed how I sit and drank some water yet the pain is getting more consistent and more painful. We decided to visit the Emergency Room for immediate assistance. On our way to the hospital, I tried to divert my attention from the chest pain to initiating a conversation with Rey. I mentioned some things that we can do that could possibly help our situation. Sadly, the simple conversation had turned into a heavy discussion that brought me to tears. It could be the tone of my voice, the way I attempted to reach understanding, and shedding light on the immediate change needed. The conversation didn't end well, rather Rey left me in the hospital as he decided to earn that night through driving service.

Over the years that we've been together and reflecting on how our relationship has evolved since we committed ourselves to anchor our relationship with God, we learned a lot about communication. We often anticipate that our over-familiarity with our spouse could automatically equate to good and peaceful communication. The truth is peaceful communication is significant in our heart condition. Our heart condition is influenced by how we perceive things. How we perceive things is dominated by the truth we choose to believe and relating to the evident sequence of circumstances. In between these connections of heart and mind, there's another truth that's commonly disregarded - the existence of the "enemy." The "enemy" will take advantage of this complicated entanglement of our hearts and minds. We will go deeper into this in Chapter 7. For now, we all know that since day one, the enemy wishes nothing but to create conflict and division among couples and families.

> *(Jesus saying), "The enemy comes only to steal and kill and destroy; I came that they may have life, and have it abundantly."* (John 10:10, NASB 1995)

The complicated entanglement of our hearts' condition doesn't automatically ensure peaceful communication. It's a consistent choice of anchoring our hearts and minds to Jesus Christ. Letting ourselves experience His authority and be transformed through His grace and mercy. As Solomon mentioned in Proverbs 21:1-2, only God can turn our hearts as He pleases. We may view ourselves in the right position but God examines our hearts.

"The king's heart is like a stream of water directed by the Lord; He guides it wherever He pleases. People may be right in their own eyes, but the Lord examines their heart." (Proverbs 21:1-2, NLT)

So, even our attempt to initiate conversation aiming for understanding and positive resolutions, will not turn out as such when our hearts are not submitted to God's authority and unwillingness to exercise our commitment in choosing Jesus Christ. It all boils down to God's will and purpose - unity under the banner of His name. So, for any changes that we anticipate and are willing to initiate, we have to submit them first to God and desire His confirmation and guidance as we commit to doing this change that will please Him and align with His will and purpose. It's not an easy thing to do but God didn't leave us alone. He sent His Son, Jesus Christ, who modeled us the submission to the authority of our God, the Father. To the point that He died on the cross for our Salvation and payment of sins. God also gifted us the Holy Spirit, who has the power to influence and take control of our minds and hearts.

Despite the seriousness of the medical condition I'm (Annie) facing, my attempt to ask help in prayers to my small group leaders was a text message that didn't fully define my complete condition that night. I was ashamed and embarrassed to acknowledge that amid such a medical emergency, Rey and I were still in conflict. My message was centered on a prayer request for my health condition. Rey returned to the hospital just in time for the doctor's initial conclusion of the findings. As well as transferring to a room that I'll be staying in for a couple of days depending on the tests' results. While still in awe of the amount of medical personnel who immediately attended to me and attached numerous monitors, my level of curiosity about my condition was not subsiding. The result of my troponin test was elevated. This measures the level of troponin T and I proteins in my blood and these proteins are released when the heart muscle has been damaged such as those that occur with a heart attack. The more damage there is to the heart, the greater the amount of troponin T and I there will be in the blood. For a person who's never been under surgery or any serious medical condition besides delivering babies, this totally surprised me and initiated fear. The busyness of the hospital during that evening led to sharing a room with a cancer patient who was just counting her days. I'm not sure of what exactly happened to her but I woke up the next day with a new cancer patient facing a life timeline as well. I just have a clear view of how life could quickly pass.

The doctors did a series of tests, but the troponin level remained high and unstable. They can't find any reason why it is elevated. The four doctors came and explained our next move. We only have one (1) test left. If that test does not give the answers that they're looking for, they will not have any other choice but to proceed with an open-heart surgery. My mouth dropped as soon as I heard the surgery. My controlled tears freely flowed down my cheeks as soon as the doctors left the room. I immediately made calls to Rey and our children. I was thinking about how I could miss their further growth if this surgery did not turn out well. I cried that night and just kept talking to God. I prayed. Then, I downloaded the Bible app on my phone and the day's verse led me to extend the reading to a whole chapter. Jesus Christ's message spoke to me;

"But seek first His kingdom and His righteousness, and all these things will be added to you. So do not worry about

29

tomorrow, for tomorrow will care for itself. Each day has
enough trouble of its own." (Matthew 6:33-34, NASB 1995)

I (Annie) meditated on these verses, and my anxiousness
suddenly turned, yielding to what God needed to tell me at
that moment. I made a few phone calls to my family and
friends. I asked for forgiveness for any pain that I've caused
them. When tiredness was about to hit my body, I used my
remaining energy by asking God. *"O God, I surrender my life
to you. If you let me leave this room, alive and be back to my family,
I will serve You.* I will offer my life in serving You." The sun
was just rising when the nurse woke me up. This time, I felt
a little excitement in her voice. She said with a full smile,
*"Mrs. Abarca, your stats are much better this morning and no
longer elevated."* I'm surprised! We still went ahead with the
scheduled test, but the surgery was no longer an option.

God showed me how I (Annie) can completely trust Him
with my life. Despite knowing God at a young age, I let Him
stay on one side of my life and not entirely in the center. I've
lived a self-sufficient life that built pride in my ability to do
things independently. My effort, hard work, and sacrifice
could deliver considerable success in my life. Yet, this time,
it's different. God showed me that my life is in His hands.
My complete dependence will no longer solely anchor on
my strength and ability but on faith and trust in God.

After Annie's heart emergency, I (Rey) noticed that her
intent in seeking God was not entirely focused on
resolutions of our circumstances alone. She sought God on
ways to serve Him. She decided to open a schedule in
starting an online women's small group. She's no longer just
an attendee in one small group. She's now initiating a small
group to facilitate. After some time, some women got
connected to her. I observed inconsistencies in some

members but I noticed Annie's firm passion in serving God. One night, her schedule just filled up and she needed to choose whether to attend the local business commerce event or her small group. She didn't want to disappoint her small group leaders, so I volunteered to be her *"proxy"* for the night. We normally attend each other's committed gathering or event if some schedule complications arise and chances permit us to do so. That night marked my official inclusion in the small group. Eventually, I met the church's pastor in charge in our region and another couple locally residing in Henderson that's also interested in starting a small group here in Las Vegas. I responded to the Gospel and accepted Jesus Christ.

Although I (Rey) accepted Jesus Christ as my personal Lord and Savior, something within is holding me to intentionally live this new life with God. There's still some blurriness on what this new life is all about. I had some questions in my mind, and I asked my wife. When I enumerated my questions, I was surprised to hear she would contact some people for help. I laughed, but I let her find help with these questions.

1. How do you forgive?
2. Why is Christianity better than other religions?
3. If there's only one God, why do we have other religions?
4. If we all come from Adam and Eve, why are there different-looking people and languages?
5. Why are aliens not mentioned in the Bible if God created the universe?

6. For those people who are gay and married with similar sex but live and follow religious beliefs, why can't they go to heaven?

7. If God wants to punish us, why do the other people around us get affected? Why not just punish the individual?

8. If you (I) live your life in a Christian way (humble, lawful, thankful, etc.), do you still get challenged every time?

9. It seems it is better to sin now and ask forgiveness later rather than live your whole life in a Christian way because you face obstacle after obstacle. Why?

10. No matter how much I prayed for my father to change when I was a child, it was never answered. How can I put my faith in God, who failed me?

Looking at these questions now, I (Rey) can't help but cry and laugh at the same time. I'm laughing because I'm happy and grateful God saved me from a perspective leading to such questions. I'm crying because I can see how I mocked God in those questions. I can see now why my wife needed to ask for help with these questions. The intentions are evident. It's not about getting direct answers or clarity; the questions are more about challenging the beliefs. I was trying to convince myself that I had made the right decision to join my wife in this new faith - Christianity. I was surprised that two (2) men took the time to answer each of my questions, and I noticed how similar their responses were. After they patiently explained everything, I still didn't end up convinced. I started reading the Bible. I want to see if their answers are really there. I intended to challenge the truth, which sparked curiosity and interest in God's words.

I ended up reading the Bible from cover to cover. Along the way, the readings led me to the thought that I can ask God if He's real. So, I asked God for a specific amount of earnings on that particular night, and He gave it to me. I asked for another amount on the second night, but getting passengers took a lot of work. It was weird as it was Friday night, and I was parked in the middle of the famous Las Vegas strip. Then I remember not opening my Bible app and reading a chapter or two. So I decided to read while waiting for passengers. After reading my chapter plan for the night, I started to receive passenger calls. I ended that night with the amount of earnings that I prayed for.

Then, one day, I (Rey) changed my prayer. I have a slip disc that requires steroid injections for every 6 to 8 months. While working in our garage, I felt this severe pain in my back, which reminded me that I was a month away from my scheduled steroid injection. Instead of setting my mind for the incoming schedule, I went to our guest room and prayed to God for healing. After the prayer, I felt this relief flowing in my body. I immediately went to see my wife and shared what God had done on my back. Then, after a couple of days of listening to numerous preachings online, I learned about contentment. I was reminded of how people often would go distant from God once their prayer is answered, and I'm indeed one of those. So I prayed to God again, but this time, I asked Him not to take my back pain totally away from me. Instead, I asked Him to let me experience it so I'll be reminded to call Him for healing. I don't want to receive complete healing and be tempted to lose my attention and focus away from God. I would rather suffer in pain than not experience His presence.

It's not just me (Rey) who was intentionally asking God to reveal Himself. The money was tight as we were going through our challenges at that time. Our children noticed the drastic changes in our lifestyle. In the middle of that adversity, we went on our knees in prayer and took the season to be closer to God. I remember one Saturday when Kira, our youngest daughter, asked my wife why we hadn't visited this famous Philippines-brand fast-food chain for a long time. My wife responded calmly that there are things we need to prioritize in our budget, and eating in restaurants will not be on our list for those days (even weeks or more in a couple of months). Then she encouraged our daughter to pray that God would provide some blessings and allow us to enjoy that food again. After that weekend, a former employee of ours gifted us a meal from that known Philippines-brand food chain on Monday. The meal was more than what she prayed for, and she didn't know that Kira was asking for it that weekend.

There were many instances in that season that helped us to solidify our faith and trust in God. He let us experience Him and have a clear look as He revealed Himself. So when He reminded me (Rey) of the unforgiveness rooted in my heart, I obeyed. I still have tears in my eyes when I ask my wife to get ready and visit my mother. During that time, I hadn't spoken to my mother for nearly a year. As my wife stayed in the parking lot, I went inside my mom's house and talked to her. I asked for forgiveness and shared with her what God had been doing in my heart. After that heartfelt meeting with my mother, we went to our warehouse but made a phone call before attending to our scheduled work. I called my father, whom I hadn't spoken to for over 20 years. His life in drug and alcohol addiction, womanizing, the suffering he gave to my mother, and my own experiences from his abusive hands had made my heart as hard as a stone towards him. Yet, at that moment, God did something in my heart that encouraged me to speak with my father and ask for forgiveness. The phone call also allowed him to ask for forgiveness for what he had done to our family. Similarly, what I did to my mother, I shared with him what God has been doing in my life. After the call, I felt a heavy burden lifted from my chest. I was crying when my wife hugged me. It was tears of relief and praising God for releasing me from such bondage of unforgiveness. Then, I told Annie that we need to share with others what God has been doing to us. I want to offer my life and serve God. You'll see more of this story in Chapter 4.

In one of the preachings that I (Annie) heard the pastor made a challenging note. If we sincerely and genuinely seek God, we could get an answer from Him in 6 months. Although he emphasized the significance of consistency and commitment, I find the mentioned time frame as a very bold challenge. My initial impression circulated on the thought that it could just be the momentary speaker's excitement. I haven't experienced speaking in that much crowd but I'm aware of the nerves that could trigger the speakers to mention some things. Although my desperation for the resolution of our overwhelming financial problem had led me to the idea that I could try it. I could and I'm willing to commit. I prayed for a specific amount of money that would completely put a dot on our problems. God didn't answer it. I checked my journal and counted the months passed. I didn't receive any significant amount of money that would help us. It brought me to tears. No! It's not because of the unanswered "way" of my prayers. He answered! It's far more valuable than the money I'm praying for. No amount can put a value on His answer. It was our hearts.

"Moreover, I will give you a new heart and put a new spirit within you; and I will remove the heart of stone from your flesh and give you a heart of flesh. I will put My Spirit within you and cause you to walk in My statutes, and you will be careful to observe My ordinances." (Ezekiel 36: 26-27, NASB1995)

Whether we look at a time frame or how we want our prayers to be answered, everything is in God's hands. It is indeed surprising when we receive His answers. Such a moment is always a great reminder of His greatness and faithfulness.

CHAPTER 3
SEEKING GOD'S DESIGN

We continue to move forward in this new life to learn more about God and incorporate Him into our marital relationship. We enjoyed our new friends - our online small group. Every session was an eye-opener as we learned from each other's struggles and testimonies. We had opportunities to get to know their stories and how God has been working in their lives - in their marital relationships. It became our spiritual family with whom we shared the same goal of anchoring our lives to Jesus Christ.

Rey & Annie's first inclusion in Couples Small Group

This group helped us be accountable in our journey with God. We've diligently spent our time with God daily - Bible reading, prayer, and meditation. As we learn more about

God, more questions are added. It was not an easy change of gear for our new identity and having God in our relationship - our family. We thought our focus and commitment to the new "spiritual" scheduled activities would lead us to the "one-way-highway" breakthroughs in our problems. We're wrong!

God has different ways and timings. The deeper we go into His words, the more we recognize rooms in our relationship that we need to work on. Indeed, the closer we come to God, the more we see the sin in ourselves. Aside from learning more about our sinful ways, there's a constant reality check that we need to deal with our current struggles. Standing amid these two is not easy; it is testing our faith. There are days that we overcome it quickly, but there are some instances when it's too much to bear, leading to disagreements and conflict. As most people would say, we're gladly taking one (1) step forward but heavily discouraged in noticing the two (2) steps backward. We felt like the clarity of this newfound life lasted for a few months, and we're drifting our ways again. We felt like we were losing our journey to this new road. We don't want to be wholly drifted away.

It took us some time to realize we needed to learn how to live this married life with God. It is not just finding God's will but completely yielding to His will and purpose as a united couple. It's no longer our desire but God's desire for us. As Galatians 2:20 says, "I have been crucified with Christ; and it is no longer I who live, but Christ lives in me.." Our responses to disappointments and frustrations were indicators that we were still holding on to something - control. We're not fully surrendering everything to God. We're having difficulty fully experiencing God because we're compartmentalizing our relationship with Him. We're compromising the relationship with Him by devoting 99% to absorbing these newly discovered truths and just allowing 1% to obedience to His truth. If we truly desire a breakthrough with Him, we must intentionally anchor every aspect of our lives to Him - 100%.

One night, we had an in-depth discussion about our relationship as husband and wife. Considering our past experiences in terms of relationships, we should have this one a lot better. Yet we noticed that we're still falling into the same trap. This time, it got more complicated because of the children and business that we shared. We realized how impactful our relationship is to every aspect of our lives - our family and our chosen lifestyle. We're becoming business partners instead of life partners. After carefully analyzing our struggles and newly developing faith, we realized that we must intentionally anchor our marital relationship to God. We both agreed that we never really had a solid standard about marriage. Just like many, we grabbed it for companionship and partnership in this life. There's nothing wrong with those objectives but there are more than those intentions. We realized that the standard we tried to establish was no longer working and just leading us to endure the relationship instead of enjoying this wonderful gift from God.

We finally decided to attend our very first Couples' Seminary. It was just a one-day event, but it was filled with so many learnings and cringe realizations. It's funny how we're so foreign to the Biblical perspective about marriage, yet the effort in the belief that it is a sacred relationship bound before God is very evident in putting importance to church weddings (still to most today). It will undoubtedly require a separate book for a thorough understanding and discussion of the Biblical perspective of marriage. Yet, for this chapter, we're sharing our learnings on the foundational truth about marriage that significantly impacted our perspective. We still remember the first time we heard about God's design for marriage and how we responded to that initial learning experience. Thus, it encouraged us to be intentional in making changes to our relationship. To this day, we're still learning and adapting to the Biblical truth about marriage. Indeed, it requires intentionality and commitment to stay focused. The noticeable progression founded by the grace of God is continually helping us to persevere. We're far from where we used to be, but there's still a lot of improvement needed to be where God intended for us.

Whenever we can share our experience on this matter, we make it clear to other couples that we're just here as witnesses, as well as to witness more of God's transformation works. We don't consider ourselves experts on this matter, and it's only by the grace of God through Jesus Christ that we're responding to His intended design for marriage. Truly it is not easy to be transformed by God's design, will, and purpose. Up to this day, we (Rey & Annie) are still learning. There's a struggle on a personal level, how much more in a marriage composed of two individuals with differences in established behaviors and perspectives. The significant changes we desire for our lives and marriages can only happen when we have Christ and move forward continuously choosing Him. As well as allowing ourselves to continuously be influenced by the power of the Holy Spirit. Because our battle is no longer in the flesh but against the powers and world forces of darkness (Ephesians 6:12), which continuously tempts us to dwell on those things that are not in obedience to God. So, it is indeed only by the grace of God that we're able to experience God's transforming power as He works (and continuously works) in our hearts. Similarly, it's a blessing to have an opportunity to witness God's transformation in many marital relationships that He allowed us to view closely. God did something in our hearts that no longer desired worldly marriage standards but His design alone. So, even when we face challenges as we persevere on God's design, by His grace, we remain focused and don't want to fall back on where we used to be. Upon hitting that road and driving ourselves to Los Angeles for this one-day couple's event, hosted by Christ Commission Fellowship (CCF) - Southern California, we look forward to learning God's blueprint in this marriage. Our mutual commitment is to equip ourselves and replace any wrong understanding and practices about marriage.

Rey & Annie's First Couples Retreat hosted by Christ Commission Fellowship (CCF) – Southern California

41

As you reach this chapter, our prayer is for God's truth to speak in your heart, and we encourage you to personally refer to the Bible to learn more about God and His design for marriage. We encourage you to refer to the Bible for the verses mentioned and reflect on the message.

What is Marriage?

There are thousands of books selling right now that talk about marriage, yet this doesn't balance out the actual status of today's marriages and family situations. The divorce rate is continuously increasing, and other heartbreaking consequences of broken marriages become more rampant and distinguishable. Marriage - its simple definition, design, and purposes got more corrupted that we find ourselves defining it in a way that will be comfortable to our personal preferences. Our relationship was a result of a wrong understanding of marriage. This mistaken understanding was based on limited knowledge and an incorrect basis. It is just driving us to the wrong path of the journey, which eventually results in endurance.

Accepting the true definition and design of marriage is impossible unless we understand and embrace the authority of God in our lives. It will be very challenging for us to replace the old understanding and be transformed into a lifestyle that God designed for us if we don't recognize the sacrifice of Jesus Christ on the cross. Otherwise, it will be challenging for our hearts to be open and our minds to articulate the Biblical perspective of marriage. So the ideal response is to initially accept Jesus Christ as personal Lord and Savior and commit to obedience unto Him in moving forward to this new life. Such decisions and declarations will stir our hearts and allow us to experience God's presence through the power of the Holy Spirit. You will experience clarity as God opens your eyes and hearts to His truth. There will be a natural hunger for His words and a genuine desire to determine the true life He intended for us.

"Then the Lord God said, 'It is not good for the man to be alone; I will make him a helper suitable for him." (Genesis 2:18, NASB1995)

The initial verse in the early part of Genesis illustrates God's intention and purpose of marriage. The Lord God determined that it was unpleasant and discomfort for the man to live alone. Whether for propagation or managing His other creations that will eventually glorify the Creator, man needs a suitable helper. The word "helper" or "helpmate" in different Bible translations has grabbed a decent amount of attention, yet also controversies. Our failure to understand the passage's complete sense has allowed many to attach this word differently. Thus, eventually, it no longer captures its true meaning and intention. The "help for the man" means "in harmony" with his nature. We set the word "help" in other forms and, most of the time, tagged to an unappealing status or identity. Yet, if we dig the Bible further, the word "help" has been used many times and is often attached to God. The careless attention to this one simple word significantly affected God's intention for us and the marriage. This carelessness eventually led us to the wrong perspective of marriage. We'll share more of this matter under the "Roles of Wives," below.

After God made a clear intention and purpose, the following verses defined His actions, demonstrating the first "marriage ceremony." This first marriage also provided a nice overview of how He intended this marriage to function - oneness.

"For this reason a man shall leave his father and his mother, and be joined to his wife; and they shall become one flesh." (Genesis 2:24, NASB1995)

Looking at details of God's creation in Genesis 1, there's a recognizable phrase: *"It was very good"* every day that He completed His work. It's not just good for Himself; God intended it for the goodness of His creations. Marriage is one of God's many good creations that unites man and woman. It is a commitment between man and woman and a covenant before God. It is designed for permanent and exclusive promise in sharing every aspect of this life.

What is God's Purpose for Marriage?

Understanding the definition of marriage from a Biblical perspective is not far from determining its purpose, and we've seen it as we dig into the above definition. Nowadays, the purpose of marriage has come in various forms for many couples. We will surely end up with a long list of reasons that developed various purposes that encouraged many of us to jump into this wagon of marriage. Now that we have a first look at marriage's Biblical perspective, we revisited that initial "purpose" that encouraged us to tie the knot. We must admit that our purpose is very far from God's. So, the first time we went deeper in learning about this Biblical perspective of marriage was an eye-opener for us. We realized that the farther our purpose is in God's design, the more we allow unnecessary things to take space in our marriage, eventually bringing nothing but complications.

Genesis 2 illustrates God's purposes in creating man, woman, and the "union." God created man and brought him to the Garden of Eden to cultivate and keep His creations. God created that man to be the overseer of His creations.

"Then the Lord God took the man and put him into the garden of Eden to cultivate it and keep it." (Genesis 12:15, NASB 1995)

In this famous story, we know that God's creation of man follows the creation of woman. We can see a clear connection of God's purpose for marriage is not far from His purpose of creating man and woman - "to cultivate and to keep." God created marriage as the union of a man and woman, suitable to each other and united in stewardship of God's other creations and blessings.

"God created man in His own image, in the image of God He created him; male and female He created them. God blessed them; and God said to them, 'Be fruitful and multiply, and fill the earth, and subdue it; and rule over the first of the sea and over the birds of the sky and over every living thing that moves on the earth." (Genesis 1:27-28, NASB1995)

Our life circumstances may bring blurriness that may affect our full comprehension of the truths in Genesis 1:27-28. These initial truths are fundamental in the foundation of our faith and marriage.

1. God created us. We're here because God gifted us a life.
2. God blessed us. This world may have set "God's blessings" in various categories and forms, but the truth is, a life in communion with Him is a blessing. Our restored relationship with God through Jesus

Christ allows us to view blessings we often missed or disregarded.

3. God commanded us to be fruitful, multiply, and be rulers (managers) of anything He entrusted us.

Following God's purpose for us also closely defines His intent for marriage. God created marriage for an impactful purpose - united in stewardship of God's entrusted creations. So, don't let this disconnection with God distract you from these beautiful truths. Stay in communion with Him to experience His purpose for you and your marriage.

God's Design for Marriage

Now that we have a better understanding of marriage and its purpose, we can refer again to Genesis 2:24 for God's intended design for marriage.

"For this reason a man shall leave his father and his mother, and be joined to his wife; and they shall become one flesh."
(Genesis 2:24, NASB1995)

Three keywords that define God's blueprint in marriage – leave, cleave, and oneness.

I.   Leave ("leave his father and his mother")

It's not in the sense that a man, upon marriage, is to cut off his affections to his parents, honoring them and neglecting their care if they need assistance. Instead, it's a clear statement of taking that wife to himself. It is a departure from the parent's household to provide their dwelling place as husband and wife. Following this initial design enables the couple to experience God's other two designs in marriage – cleave and oneness.

46

II. Cleave ("be joined to his wife")

Cleave is an intentional change of priorities for the spouse. The husband's top priority is now his wife. Some theologians defined this phrase in the following;

1. Taking care of the wife
2. Nourishing and cherishing her
3. Providing for her
4. Continuously living with her and not departing from her

Together with "leave," God's intention for marriage is permanent and requires total commitment to honor the marriage covenant.

III. Oneness ("they shall become one flesh")

The oneness here speaks for the intimate union of husband and wife, which results in emotional, spiritual, and physical-body oneness. The married couple shall no longer have separate interests but act as if they were one.

The three factors of God's design for marriage may look quite simple and direct. Yet complexity may arise when we live apart from God's design. The objections wrapped with justification are very evident in today's generation. We're surprised to learn that the objection exists even in times of the Old Testament. God made it clear in Malachi 2:16 that He hates divorce. Another discussion of this matter was recorded in the New Testament when some Pharisees tested Jesus Christ and asked Him about divorce in Matthew 19:3-9.

When we discussed the topic of divorce in the Couples' Seminar, we were confused about how to respond. We understood God's objection to it and how firm His instruction was over it. What about us? Our marriage is the third from the previous line of 2 divorces. Where are we going to put ourselves now? Thank God for our spiritual group and leaders as they help us navigate this truth. The divorces and remarriage happened when we're living a life away from God. Now that we're fully aware of this truth and explained to us clearly, divorce no longer exists (even in a manner of consideration) in our marriage. Knowing this truth added another layer of gratefulness to Jesus Christ. It's part of the sin that was paid off when Jesus Christ died on that cross. Now, we have a new life with greater hope and embracing God's blessing of marriage.

Roles in Marriage

Part of God's design for marriage also covers the roles of the two individuals united in this covenant. From the beginning that God created Adam, there's an explicit instruction of his role - to oversee God's other creations. When God noticed that it was not for a man to be alone, Eve was created. In this simple sequence of events, we can conclude that God created man and woman for specific roles. Going further in the story, the word "helper" was first introduced. This word described in Genesis 2:18 supported the recognition of roles in marriage. This "role" matter could be a very tricky topic and challenging to grasp. If you've heard about this before and ended up asking more questions, don't worry. We experienced the same way, too! As the Bible unveils our roles in this marriage, we're collecting more questions in mind. The "pattern" we grew up with and adapted in our marital relationship is far from

God's defining roles. Our initial responses show that the truths incorporated in this matter are far from what we used to believe and witnessed in others. As we've given time to process the learnings and discussed the collected questions formed upon listening to the truth, we realized that the "roles" indeed make sense. The evident difference between men and women proceeds on distinct roles, yet both are equally important. How we wish there was a university course that detailed marriage, its purpose, and most importantly, the roles of husband and wife, yet none! This can only be found in the Bible. It's a blessing for us to determine that these teachings exist, and it's another blessing if we yield to them wholly and accordingly. Come to think of it, the farther we let ourselves and our marriage away from God's truth, the more we invite confusion, which will eventually lead to conflicts and destruction. When we heard about these roles, we took our first step in responding to the truth by opening our hearts to it.

The roles of husbands and wives were further expounded in the writings of Apostle Paul in Ephesians 5. This chapter is known for studying the husband-wife relationship. However, for us, it was only in that first couple's seminar that we learned about this. Surprisingly funny yet dangerously sad, how in our previous lives we were decently exposed to the Bible, yet we didn't have any chance to stumble on this nor give serious attention to it.

Roles of Husbands

1. Leader

Ephesians 5:23 noted a good sequence of God's order in family and church. It is also supported in 1 Corinthians 11:3.

"For the husband is the head of the wife, as Christ is the head of the church, He, Himself being the Savior of the body." (Ephesians 5:2, NASB1995)

"But I want you to understand that Christ is the head of every man, and the man is the head of a woman, and God is the head of Christ." (1 Corinthians 11:3, NASB995)

The order illustrated in these two verses is very consistent in the event of creation in Genesis 2. We've learned the responsibilities entrusted to man by God towards the other creations. This responsibility continues to the woman who was created for him. Therefore, the man must be the head and leader to the woman gifted to him and in any other affairs or blessings God provided in this marriage. We can also determine in the above verses the type of leadership that God intended for man to practice in marriage, which is - just like Christ as the head of the church and God as the head of Christ. Jesus Christ famously exercised grace, mercy, and love to the church - to His body. As well as the great obedience of Jesus Christ to God, the Father. Jesus Christ committed Himself to God even in death. The husband's role doesn't just centralize the authority towards the wife but significantly recognizes his submission to the authority of Jesus Christ on him.

This role normally triggers a lot of conversation with many, particularly with couples who will hear it for the first time. Annie and I (Rey) certainly have a different reaction from the first time we learned about it and today we'd got time for further digging about it. I can certainly say that this role has been corrupted in my ways by this world, which just tells us that we attached in fulfilling this role is our great dependence on God, the modeling of Christ, and the influence of the Holy Spirit.

2. Lover

This is the husband's second role, as specified in this portion of Ephesians 5.

"Husbands, love your wives, just as Christ loved the church and gave Himself up for her." (Ephesians 5:25, NASB1995)

Like the leadership role, love here refers to Jesus Christ's love for the church. Apostle Paul did mention some practical notes that describe this "love."

"So husbands ought also to love their own wives as their own bodies. He who loves his own wife loves himself. For no one ever hated his own, but nourishes and cherishes it." (Ephesians 5:28-29, NASB1995)

Far from what "love" is commonly promoted out there. It is an action towards someone; in this case, it is the husband towards the wife. Treating the wife as an extension of the husband oneself and the two key words "nourishes and cherishes." Naturally, man constantly nourishes and cherishes their body by protecting or healing from hurt which is generally centered on welfare and comfort. Thus, husbands must act towards their wives and relate it to Jesus Christ's love towards the church. We all know how He gave Himself for the church. He may show anger or great disapproval of the sin but not of the person. His love is everlasting and unchangeable. He nourishes the church towards maturity and cherishes the church by granting them an intimate communion with Himself.

Roles of Wives

1. Helper/Helpmate Suitable to Husband

God made it clear in Genesis 2:18 that He intended the wives to be "helpers suitable" for the husbands. The phrase "help meet for him" is from the Greek word *êzer* [3] , a most significant phrase which means a man's counterpart suitable to his nature and his need. She's a "help/helper" to a man, which most experts explained as being at hand, or near to him, to converse familiarly with him and always be ready to comfort him. The wives' main case and business is to please and help the husbands.

This role truly triggered many reactions, particularly among wives. When I (Annie) first heard about this "helpmate" role, I realized that I would have a challenge to obey God in this design. I may be able to do it, but would certainly in clear boundaries. I know I will encounter similar reactions from fellow wives, especially those who will hear it for the first time. However as I dug deeper into this particular term, I learned that the Hebrew-Aramaic word for this is in similar usage found in other 21 verses, and some are in reference to God, like in Psalm 33:20, Psalm 70:5, Psalm 115:11, and Psalm 115:9 [4] . Not in the sense of "helper" but God provided help to the Israelites, which He is still doing to our needs today. This truth could trigger different contexts and may lean toward superiority or be taken in supporting the description of higher value.

---

[3] NAS Exhaustive Concordance of the Bible with Hebrew-Aramaic and Greek Dictionaries, 1981,1998. *Lockman Foundation.* www.lockman.org

[4] NAS Exhaustive Concordance of the Bible with Hebrew-Aramaic and Greek Dictionaries, 1981,1998. *Lockman Foundation.* www.lockman.org

If we let ourselves fall into such a perspective, then we're disregarding the other truth that's commanding our husbands to be our leader and it will be contracting the Apostle Paul's words in Ephesians 5:23. So for me (Annie), I took this in the sense of how important it is for us, wives, to be in great dependence on God for this role (as well as on the others). We should be intentional in grounding ourselves in the influence of the Holy Spirit so that our response to this role will remain in the boundary that honors all of His other commands and designs.

2. Submit

"Submit" or "Submission" evidently will easily create controversies and confusion when taken in context away from the relationship of the other verses in this chapter. Or even farther from the creation story in Genesis 2.

"Wives, be subject to your own husbands, as to the Lord." (Ephesians 5:22, NASB1995)

In other translations, "be subject" is "submit." Following the readings to verse 24, the submission pertains to "in everything." This submission is not subject to unequal importance. Let's remind ourselves that the message of the Gospel secures the equal importance of man and woman. On the other hand, the submission of wives to husbands recognizes and secures man's leadership responsibility in the marriage.

3. Respect

The last verse of Ephesians 5 illustrates the different language of love between husband and wife, yet significantly related compared to the love of Jesus Christ for the church.

"Nevertheless, each individual among you also is to love his own wife even as himself, and the wife must see to it that she respects her husband." (Ephesians 5:33, NASB1995)

In some Bible translations, "respect" is translated as "reverence." Theologians explain this act of reverence towards the husband as fear not with a servile (or excessive willingness, which characterizes enslaved people) but rather an honest and trusting fear that proceeds from love.

Apostle Paul's writings in Ephesians 5 presented a very good note for the roles of husbands and wives. What's so interesting in the flow of this chapter is that it started with the teachings for the church to become imitators of God (Ephesians 5:1-21). The entire chapter's narrative clearly supports the idea that God's design for marriage is not possible away from Jesus Christ. Today, we're blessed with many churches and non-profit organizations that offer marriage seminars and retreats based on Biblical truths added with real-life testimonies of other couples. After attending the 1-day Marriage Retreat in Los Angeles, we also attended other marriage seminars that detailed the Biblical design of marriage. Whenever there's an opportunity, we're always excited to relearn and hear more of couples' testimonies.

The Biblical perspective of marriage could be overwhelming and sometimes could lead us to a confusing path on where to begin. We felt that too! Yet what spoke strongly to us upon discovering these truths is God's mercy. Reassessing ourselves, our past choices, and the timing of knowing these truths could have shed more disastrous consequences on us. Yes, we're having some challenges but God's mercy has let us view these truths as enlightenment and a great blessing. God's grace through Jesus Christ brought encouragement and great hope to the transformation of our marriage.

So, don't be discouraged in seeing your marriage far distant from God's design; instead, be excited about God's transforming power and work.

CHAPTER 4
EMBRACING DISCIPLESHIP

We've never had a chance to take a deeper account of our discipleship journey until we received God's conviction in writing this book. Between the two of us, our life circumstances before are nowhere near to being an author. So when God strongly impressed this in us, our resistance leaned on to not having a decent study or experience in writing a book. Yet our commitment to serving God is primarily being used as His witnesses that Jesus Christ is alive and continuously transforming lives. Our efforts in concluding the initial outline of this book led us to the importance of sharing the stories with collective testimonies from relearning, restoration, and rejoicing. The story must include our defining moment in this discipleship journey and its significance in our continuing walk today.

Discipleship is commonly and popularly shared through Matthew 28: 19-20, which covers the what and how of discipleship.

> *"Go therefore and make disciples of all the nations, baptizing them in the name of the Father and the Son and the Holy Spirit, teaching them to observe all that I commanded you; and lo, I am with you always, even to the end of the age."*
> (Matthew 28: 19-20, NASB 1995)

The basics of discipleship were covered by these two verses;

1. The word "Go" denotes a commandment and the required motion from our end.

2. The word "therefore" relates and highlights the importance of discipleship to the act of Jesus Christ on the cross and rising from death. The enumerated story in the whole chapter of Matthew 28 provided a clear conclusion on this command.

3. The "All the nation" phrase defines the extent of discipleship beyond geographical borders.

4. The clarity and acceptance of the Gospel are necessary for this discipleship journey as verse 19 says, "baptizing them in the name of the Father, the Son, and the Holy Spirit."

5. Discipleship is a heart of all the teachings and obedience to God's commands - *"teaching them to observe all that I commanded you"*

6. We should and must stand firm against the challenges along the way with the promise of Jesus Christ - *"and lo, I am with you always, even to the end of the age."*

Indeed, a complete overview of discipleship and the excitement incorporated in this movement appeals to many. Its powerful message awakens many sleeping souls who have been waiting to live a life with a purpose, just like us!

The first time I (Annie) heard discipleship, I knew I needed it and it was important. My early exposure to the message of the Gospel which could have been a great help in my teen years wasn't firm enough to not let myself escape from making some wrong choices. Thus leading me to a journey of so-called "double life." Come to think of it, it is indeed a shameful journey. Yet, my renewal of faith has viewed that past season through the lens of God's amazing grace. I could have ended in a more disastrous situation, but

God reminded me of His protection and grace in many of my previous "critical moments." It teared me up to think that I took God for granted in those years, yet He remained in protecting my well-being. I was exposed to drinking, smoking, and even premarital sex but God lovingly reminded me of His existence from time to time. He provided on the needs for completion of my education, which led me to good work opportunities. I wasn't planning to leave the Philippines, yet God allowed me to experience life in other places that I never imagined. When I was in college, I used to keep a collage of pictures of a life that I dreamed of. A picture of a family with a decent house and a car that will fit a family of five. God granted me that "family", even the specific type of car I wanted! When God allowed me to remember that motivational craft work, He made sure that I recognized His works. Indeed God never fails. He will never forsake us.

Looking at further details of that journey, I can easily tell that it was not smooth, and many of the wrong turns were the choices I (Annie) made. Choices that weren't surrendered to God nor sought His guidance and approval. Remembering those years will certainly trigger me to feel ashamed and embarrassed, but God's mercy spoke louder and stronger. So for someone like me who once strongly connected with God but gone astray, discipleship is the key. We're not created to be a lone ranger in this life journey. God wants us to be surrounded by fellow believers and Christ-followers who will journey with us and collectively be encouraged to exercise our Salvation and keep pursuing Christ Jesus. Indeed, you need to stay engaged through discipleship after accepting Jesus Christ as your personal Lord and Savior.

On the other hand, I (Rey) didn't have the same heart position about discipleship similar to Annie's. The first time I heard the phrase, *"I will disciple you,"* my mind set on the thought that I would be told on what to do. Despite their efforts in explaining it clearly, my heart and mind remained in the understanding that discipleship is to be "fixed" by someone and not by God. So, the early season that I was joining Annie in the small group and listening to Sunday Messages was focused more on my questions and curiosity. My suspicion about these new people that Annie was letting into our lives has led me to find answers to my questions directly to the Bible. I'm not a reader, and I never finish a book, even when I was studying in school. Yet there's something in the Bible that captured my attention and kept me engaged. As I continued reading the Bible, God's message on surrendering my life to Him was speaking loudly and clearly. The resistance was strong and even today I can't find the right words to describe what I was feeling and thinking then. It's like a mixture of doubts and great resistance that God is alive and touching people's hearts today. My continuous reading has encouraged me to ask God to reveal Himself, and He ensured that I (and my family) recognized Him. We started to collect stories that, even today, we're still in awe of how God orchestrated things. I initially shared this in Chapter 2. The two consecutive nights that I specifically prayed for earnings in that driving service I used to do and He gave me those in exact value. I witnessed the excitement and joy that Annie and our children shared when God answered our prayers. Indeed, God's revelations were very convincing when making a decision, and I did!

I (Rey) decided to ask Him for a "pause"! I stopped reading the Bible and listening to praise and worship songs in the remaining few days of 2018. I took the "pause" to further reevaluate myself and this growing connection with God. I asked Him for some space, and I have such pride. My request for a "pause" lasted for 4 days. I didn't know that I was in the middle of spiritual warfare at that moment. Yet, I thanked God for His grace and the power of the Holy Spirit that He didn't let me be completely taken away by Satan.

Early morning on that 5th day of that "pause", while still in bed, Annie and I were engaged in a text messaging exchange with her side of the family. Annie tried to share forgiveness and encourage her family to end conflicts. As I witnessed the exchange of words, I decided to dive into the conversation. While expressing my thoughts, I felt something different flowing in my body that I can't explain. My eyes overflowed with tears as I continued to articulate those words about forgiveness. My thoughts were shared with them, but my tears showed that I needed to take those words to myself first. I stood up and asked Annie to prepare herself. It's about time to take action and end these "pause" days. The rest of that day was spent in reconciliation with my parents. The heavy burden that's lifted from my heart has finally freed and opened me to commit to following Christ, surrendering my life, and serving Him. I told Annie that we need to share our experience with others and start with the discipleship locally. It was the day that I fully embraced God's command of discipleship.

We're thankful for God's orchestration, that when He called our attention to surrendering our lives to Him and embracing discipleship, our life's situation paved the way to obey such command in our relationship as husband and wife, then to our children. When I (Rey) noticed the changes in Annie, I told her that we could focus on discipleship and work together to share what we learned with our children. At first, she was hesitant, thinking our young children would struggle to adjust. Annie pointed out the established schedule we've placed from our weekly "religious activities," such as attending a local church, sending kids to Children's Sunday School, and even their inclusion during summer camps. There's nothing wrong with those activities. It could be helpful at some point, but falling on the temptation to rely alone on these "religious activities" and not doing anything that follows God's design for engaging our children (Proverbs 22:6, Ephesians 6:4, Deuteronomy 6:1-9) may require a sincere heart-check for us parents if we truly desire to obey God. At the end of the day, the best influence should still be coming from us - the parents. The Lord God gifted them to us (Psalm 127:3), and our stewardship of these blessings includes our commitment to guide them to Christ and God's teachings. Together, we made bold changes in our schedule and lifestyle. We started by having a conversation with our children about the change. Initially, Annie and I asked our children's forgiveness for our parenting that wasn't following Biblical principles. Then, the conversation led to sharing the gospel by using John 3:16, and Annie's teaching skills helped me share the message that's appropriate to their ages.

As expected, they were surprised, yet eventually, our family adapted to this new lifestyle. It wasn't an easy transition for all of us, the only thing that constantly motivates us (Rey & Annie) is our fear of God.

Rey sharing the Gospel with their children

Our commitment to continuously share Christ with our children is our way of surrendering them to Him. We know we have limitations and we constantly remind them that in the end, it's their choice to have that personal connection with Christ. Our constant prayer is for God to equip us, as we continue with this commitment in every season of our children's lives.

When we opened our home to other people interested in discipleship, we had only our experience with the Gospel message, collection of testimonies, and commitment to obey God's command. We knew we had to learn more and were not equipped for this. I (Rey) used to say, *"I didn't sign up for this,"* whenever there were misunderstandings or complications. Yet, our heart to obey God encouraged us to make ourselves available and move forward in encouraging others for family discipleship.

We didn't anticipate the number of people who would be interested in being part of this. We witnessed how God started and kept sending people along our way. As we get to know more people, the more we see a collection of unique stories, and we're starting to see inadequacy in ourselves. Our early season of discipleship has led us to the reality that it is indeed God's program, not ours - neither an established organization. Just like in our marriage, we noticed a similar season in which we got to know God, committed ourselves to the message of the Gospel, and experienced the moving conviction of the Holy Spirit to obey His commands. Although those experiences didn't automatically fall at the same time. There were gaps and differences. It would be a great blessing that the couple will experience the acceptance of the Gospel and commitment to discipleship at the same and the same level of commitment. It didn't go in ours and we observed similarities to many people we've met and encountered. Indeed, we all have unique stories, but the foundation of Christ is the same. So, the idea and perception of discipleship as a program, a scheduled curriculum, or Bible Study alone is far different from its true essence.

In one of Jim Daly's ReFocus podcast episodes, there's an interview with [5] Dave Boden, the author of the book *"Parallel Faith: Walking Alongside Others on Their Journey to Christ,"* he said;

> *"Before you become a discipler, be a disciple first. Say yes to Jesus Christ first. We will never ever make a disciple until we realize that there's so much by just being a church-goer."*(Dave Boden)

---

[5] Boden, D. [Author - Parallel Faith: Walking Alongside Others On Their Journey to Christ]. (n.d.). *Doing life with others while sharing Christ* (J. Daly [ReFocus With Jim Daly], Interviewer). https://tinyurl.com/RefocusDaveBoden

Discipleship is a life anchored in Jesus Christ, and sharing with others is an invitation to a "shared" journey. Before you become a discipler or disciple-maker, you need to be a disciple first. Our common mistake is equating the phrase "being a disciple first" directly to being attached to a small group (or being a member) alone! There should be a clear understanding, declaration, and definition of the Gospel. Timothy Keller shared that being a disciple of Jesus Christ means (1) setting a new priority (Luke 9:57-62), (2) finding a new identity (Luke 9:23-25), and (3) living a new mercy (Luke 9) [6]. Indeed being a disciple is a commitment to following Jesus Christ in this life journey and learning to obey all God's commands toward Christlikeness. The usual impression is sharing this discipleship journey in a small group, but this could take place in a marital relationship or even the entire family in a household.

The response of passing discipleship to others results from God's conviction of obedience to His command that's clearly expressed in your heart and mind.

The word "therefore" in Matthew 28:19 is very profound. It is not just a reminder of the real essence of discipleship, but it's our defining moment - a life-changing moment; (1) understanding and acceptance of the Gospel, (2) opening our lives to experience the power of the Holy Spirit, particularly during the sanctification process, and (3) a new life that's blessed with the God's presence. Truly, the word "therefore" is life-changing.

---

[6] Keller, T. (2011). The Call to Discipleship. *C.S. Lewis Institute.* https://www.cslewisinstitute.org/

The avenue of discipleship and active participation in small groups helped us better understand the Gospel and a new life with Christ. Our initial intuition of coming to Christ is to save ourselves and our young family from our difficult situation. Although we all know that obedience to God comes with blessings, it's different when the so-called "blessings" are wrongly defined in your mind and heart. It could turn into an object of idol, and the inclusion of Christ in our lives could turn into a give-and-take transaction. So our early season in discipleship has led us to a good understanding of who God is and the definition of His blessings. The last part in Matthew 28:20, *"and lo, I am with you always, even to the end of the age,"* emphasizes the continuity of Christ's presence. The coming days might seem challenging, even long, dark, and deary, but He, our God, will be with us each day. There will be assistance in doing His will in our roles in this life, comfort under all discouragements, supplication of grace, protection against "enemies," and preservation from all evils. Indeed, it is a great encouragement. Who are we to question such a wonderful promise from Jesus Christ?

Despite Christ's amazing promise, there's an undeniable recognition of hesitation to discipleship. Our lives that once separated from God, added with the brokenness of this world, attract more of our attention to the phrase *"observe all that I commanded you."* The "obedience" that is supposedly a gear to our new life favored by God became a critical choice against sacrifices in following Christ (Luke 9:23-24, Luke 13:24, Luke 14:27-28). We may have accepted the message of the Gospel because our whole being is screaming for help for His power to improve our lives. Yet discipleship will define our true relationship with Jesus Christ - do we truly accept Him as our personal Lord and Savior?

In Ephesians 2, Apostle Paul outlines the three major barriers to following Christ - the world, the flesh, and the devil. If those are blocking us from following Christ, they're also blocking us from obeying and sharing the true essence of discipleship.

"And you were dead in your trespasses and sins, in which you formerly walked according to the course of this world, according to the prince of the power of the air, of the spirit that is now working in the sons of disobedience. Among them, we too all formerly lived in the lusts of our flesh, indulging the desires of the flesh and of the mind, and were by nature children of wrath, even as the rest." (Ephesians 2:1-3, NASB1995)

Mr. Thomas A. Tarrants III, who served as Director of Ministry at CS Lewis Institute, released a nice 4-part series article entitled, *"Hindrances to Discipleship,"* noted;

"..they (world, flesh, and evil) interact with one another to create a challenging array of problems, internal and external, for every disciple." [7] (Thomas Tarrants III)

Moral blindness will always exist until we understand the bondages that hold us in these three hindrances. The same blindness could lead us on a life journey that would cause us to miss the wonderful blessing of discipleship.

---

[7] Tarrants, T. III (2012). Hindrances to Discipleship. *C.S. Lewis Institute.* https://www.cslewisinstitute.org/

In the remainder of this chapter, we'll share what we learned about these hindrances, emphasizing the context of marriage and its significance in our personal walk of faith.

Hindrances to Discipleship: The World

The initial negative impression of the "world" is marked by Adam and Eve's story. When the Lord sent them out from the garden of Eden, they were sent to a place where they needed "to cultivate the ground" (Genesis 3:22-24). The Bible may not indicate the exact location, but the verse gave us a good impression that it's a place where hard labor occurs. This signifies the difference in their living status in the garden, which we can also see in more detail in Genesis 3:16-17. After such, the Bible has detailed numerous experiences in this "world" and the various uses of the word "world." If we do not pay good attention to context details, we will find ourselves confused about how God's wonderful creation has this negative impression. But come to think of it, the complexity of the word "world" usage in the Bible just gives us a good sense of idea and awareness to be careful when treating this word and sincerely reflect on how it's affecting us.

Following the article that[8] Mr. Tarrants released, he mentioned that the most significant Greek word used, which translates as "world," is kosmos, which originally meant "order or arrangement" (Matthew 12:44, Luke 11:25).

---

[8] Tarrants, T. III (2012). Hindrances to Discipleship. *C.S. Lewis Institute.* https://www.cslewisinstitute.org/

The related verb is kosmeó [9] which means to order or arrange (Matthew 23:29, Luke 21:5, 1 Timothy 2:9, 1 Peter 3:5). According to Dr. Robert Bratcher,[10] a Bible Translator, noted that the noun kosmos occurs some 188 times in the New Testament, of which 104 are in the Gospel and the Letters of John. Another 46 times, the word appears in Apostle Paul's letters and the so-called Pastoral Letters (1 and 2 Timothy, Titus). Dr. Bratcher also noted;

> *"The idea of order is always present in the meaning 'universe' or 'world,' which is the sense the Greek noun most often carries. In biblical thought, of course, this order is the result of God's activity. God created the universe as an orderly, harmonious system."*

For furthermore understanding, we can refer to how[11] Dr. Bratcher organized the translation of the Greek word kosmos in the following contexts;

- The Universe - the whole creation (Acts 17:24)

- This World - the place in which we live, the earth (Romans 4:13, Matthew 4:8, Matthew 13:38; 26:13, Mark 16:15)

- Humanity - the people who live on earth (John 1:10;1:29;3:16-17, Matthew 5:14; 18:7)

- The Worldly Activities and Values - corrupt and evil activities (Matthew 16:26, 1 John 2:15-16, Colossians 2:20)

---

[9] Strong's Concordance. (n.d.). Greek Translation. In *Bible Hub*. https://www.biblehub.com

[10] Robert G. Bratcher, "The meaning of kosmos, 'world', in the New Testament," *Bible Translator* 31.4 (Oct. 1980): 430-434.www.biblestudies.org.uk

[11] Robert G. Bratcher, "The meaning of kosmos, 'world', in the New Testament," *Bible Translator* 31.4 (Oct. 1980): 430-434.www.biblestudies.org.uk

Although Dr. Bratcher was able to organize the major meaning of kosmos in the New Testament, he found the two passages that were hard to fit the meaning in the above selections;

- (1 Corinthians 8:4) *"Therefore concerning the eating of things sacrificed to idols, we know that there is no such thing as an idol in the world and that there is no God but one."*

  ○ It is evident that Apostle Paul is emphasizing the nothingness of the idol - not in the sense of its existence (such as a block of wood, carved image, or any object of worship), but in comparison to the power of God. So, following Dr. Bratcher's identification, "in the world" seems to mean "real" or "actual."[12] A Bible commentator said the phrase "in the world" seems just to be added by way of emphasis - to show the utter nothingness of idols.

- (James 3:6) "And the tongue is a fire, the very world of iniquity; the tongue is set among our members as that which defiles the entire body, and sets on fire the course of our life, and is set on fire by hell."

  ○ [13]The writer of this verse equated the tongue with "the very world of iniquity," which doesn't directly refer to the tongue itself but to its activity. Thus, it seems the phrase "world of iniquity" seems to mean an organized system of evil.

---

[12] Barnes' Notes on the Bible.. In *Bible Hub*. https://www.biblehub.com
[13] Robert G. Bratcher, "The meaning of kosmos, 'world', in the New Testament," *Bible Translator* 31.4 (Oct. 1980): 430-434.www.biblestudies.org.uk

Looking at these experts' studies and Bible verses, there's a clear conclusion that the "world" is God's creation but contains brokenness and sin. It's a place or condition where temptation exists, and our volition matters. It could be the state of our separation from God (in reference to the Adam-Eve story and the historical continuity of sin today), but it doesn't equate to the fact that His authority will no longer exist. God sent His Son, Jesus Christ, to save us in this world and restore our connection to our Creator. Aside from Christ's modeling and authority (Matthew 28:18), the Holy Spirit will help us navigate this life anchored in God. Moral blindness starts when we allow ourselves to continually live separated from God, navigate this life away from His authority, and lean more into the negative shade meaning of this "world."

I (Annie) didn't realize how deeply influenced I was by this "world" until I discovered and learned the Biblical perspectives on the roles that God entrusted to me. Despite my sincere intention of being Rey's "good" life partner, I let to explore such intention away from God and His words. We may have a good understanding of how we'd continue this life in the family context. Our shared goals from home management, parenting, and even enjoying the pleasures of life as a couple may be acceptable in the culture and evidently paralleled in the pattern we've seen in this world. It was a season that God was totally out of the picture and discussion. We never consulted His design, will, and purpose. I was eager to prepare the kids from infancy to a certain age that I could entrust them. Take advantage of freedom in between and start paying attention to establishing a new life in this new habitat while they are growing. Not knowing that as we let more days to let them navigate this world without any foundational connection to God, we're digging ourselves into deeper consequences of a life unanchored in Him. In addition, our wrong perspective of success and the true essence of life led us to fall into the evil scheme here in the world. We shared the organized details of this in Chapter 1.

Our children were already at ages 6, 10, and 14 when we finally took action in God's call, and we knew we only had a few years and spaces left to change the foundation of our parenting. Besides the complications of our wrong choices and the effect of past mistakes, we have much to learn and replace our non-Biblical parenting. They've also witnessed in us a life away from God. Things would be different if we'd taken action much sooner and grounded ourselves in God's words - even on the day we committed ourselves to this marriage. We knew we were walking under God's mercy on all these catch-ups, even today, as we committed ourselves to moving forward. Yet, God is faithful, and His grace is sufficient. God gave us a chance to share the gospel with them. God helped us to change our engagement with them as we embraced homeschooling when the COVID-19 pandemic happened. We got a chance to collect testimonies as a family, and they've witnessed how God sustained us during challenging and difficult times, leaning on Him. Christianity was not "sugar-coated" in our household. Our children witnessed the reality of sacrifices in following Christ because of our love for Him. Family discussions have changed, even though there were moments when our "old" behavior tempted us, we managed to anchor ourselves back to God's grace and mercy. Today, we're still learning about our parenting roles to our children. We pray that they remember every moment we've encountered God, not just in good times but in every struggle that our family relied on His grace, mercy, and love. May every testimony not be forgotten as they begin navigating their lives in this world's complexity. Indeed Christianity is impossible in this world apart from Christ and the power of the Holy Spirit. Just like what [14] Mr. Tarrants said;

> *"The world is, therefore, a battleground in which a war rages between God and the devil, seen in the struggle in between good and evil, truth and error, life and death. And the devil and his forces work relentlessly and skillfully to seduce and ensnare people with the godless values of this fallen world. We cannot escape being in this world, but we can and must avoid being of it."*

Although the details and reality of the "world" may drive us to view life anchored in Christ as challenging, let's be encouraged to stay connected and strongly dependent on Him. Just like the Apostle Paul said;

> *"Therefore I urge you, brethren, by the mercies of God, to present your bodies a living and holy sacrifice, acceptable to God, which is your spiritual service of worship. And do not be conformed to this world, but be transformed by the renewing of your mind, so that you may prove what the will of God is, that which is good and acceptable and perfect."* (Romans 12:1-2, NASB1995)

Hindrances to Discipleship: The Flesh

Just like the "world," the word "flesh" is used in various ways in the Bible, and its meaning is determined by the context in which it appears.

---

[14] Tarrants, T. III (2012). Hindrances to Discipleship. *C.S. Lewis Institute.* https://www.cslewisinstitute.org/

There's a clear recognition of commonality in this term that familiarity exists even for a person who's not regularly diving into God's words or listening to Biblical messages. Although our familiarity doesn't directly equate to a full understanding of this word. [15] Mr. Thomas A. Tarrants III noted a very strong yet profound statement that could lead us to sincerely check our heart and life concerning the word "flesh."

> *"Although the word flesh is fairly common among believers, our understanding of it is often shallow and limited. Frequently it is used as a synonym for sexual lust instead of as the fallen human nature that controls nonbelievers and seeks to control believers. This misunderstanding is a serious problem for those who want to live for Christ; if we don't understand the flesh rightly, we cannot rightly understand sin and how to deal with it."*(Thomas A. Tarrants III)

Such a statement truly applies to us, and it encouraged us to be more aware of determining the meaning of "flesh" in the context in which it was used in a chapter (even with the entire book). The daily meditation and reflection on God's words truly provide an understanding of its connection and relation to our lives today. Yet our self-awareness and desire to further go deeper into God's word impact our continuous walk of life under God's authority. Just like in the word "flesh," our intentionality to follow Christ should encourage us to expand our knowledge of its meaning and learn how it operates and affects us. Surely it will require further space to dive completely into the meaning of "flesh."

---

[15] Tarrants, T. III (2012). Hindrances to Discipleship. *C.S. Lewis Institute.* https://www.cslewisinstitute.org/

We're sharing detailed notes that helped us not get lost when encountering this word in the Old or New Testaments. After such, we'll share how this knowledge determination helped us understand the significant effect of "flesh" in our desire to follow Christ.

Before diving straight to the New Testament for the word "flesh," it's good that we don't ignore how this word was used in the Old Testament. [16] Dr. Robert Bratcher released a comprehensive translation of "Flesh." In the Old Testament, "flesh" is from the Hebrew word bâsâr and has several meanings;

- It refers to the material of which living beings (animal and human) are made (Genesis 40:19; 2 Kings 9:36)

- It can also mean the body (1 Kings 21:27; Numbers 19:7)

- In some passages means the self, the whole person "I" (Psalms 16:9-10)

- The phrase "all flesh" means all living creatures (Genesis 6:17, 7:15-16) or all living human beings (Genesis 6:12; Psalms 145:21)

- To indicate close relationship and kinship: husband and wife (Genesis 2:23-24); family (Genesis 29:14); clan (Judges 9:2); race (2 Samuel 5:10)

- To characterize man as weak, mortal, and frail, especially in contrast with God, who is all-powerful (Psalms 56:4, Psalms 78:39)

---

[16] Robert G. Bratcher, "The Meaning of sarx ('flesh') in Paul's letters," *Bible Translator* 29.2 (April 1978): 212-218.www.biblicalstudies.org.uk

In the New Testament, [17] the word "flesh" is from the Greek word sarx, which is used 147 times, 91 of which are from the writings of the Apostle Paul. It is also used in different ways. [18] Dr. Batcher also presented a good list with corresponding Bible verses;

- Flesh - of which living beings are composed: "All sarx is not the same sarx" (1 Corinthians 15:39): "all flesh," all people (Romans 3:20; Galatians 2:16; 1 Corinthians 1:29): "flesh and blood" (1 Corinthians 15:50; Galatians 1:16; 1; Ephesians 6:12)
- The Body - the physical self, the body
  - The word is used in passages in which the subject is circumcision (Romans 2:28; Galatians 6:12-13; Colossians 2:13; Ephesians 2:11)
  - In the sexual union of man and woman that become "one flesh" (Genesis 2:24, quoted in 1 Corinthians 6:16; Ephesians 5:28-31)
  - The word is used for bodily presence (Colossians 2:1,5; 1 Corinthians 5:3)
  - It can refer to physical infirmity (Galatians 4:13-14; 2 Corinthians 12:7)
  - It also refers to physical toil, experience, and suffering (Colossians 1:24; 2 Corinthians 4:10-11)
  - The whole person can be described as "flesh and spirit" (2 Corinthians 7:1; 1 Corinthians 5:5)

---

[17] Tarrants, T. III (2012). Hindrances to Discipleship. *C.S. Lewis Institute.* https://www.cslewisinstitute.org/

[18] Robert G. Bratcher, "The Meaning of *Sarx* ('flesh') in Paul's letters," *Bible Translator* 29.2 (April 1978): 212-218.www.biblicalstudies.org.uk

- This life, bodily existence, is lived "in the flesh" (Galatians 2:20; 2 Corinthians 10:3; Philippians 1:22,24)
- Passages Referring to Christ
  - (Romans 8:3) that God sent His Son "in the likeness of sinful flesh," which means that Christ was fully human, except that He was not sinful
  - (Ephesians 2:14-15) that Christ broke down the wall of separation "in His flesh" (His physical existence)
  - (Romans 1:3) that Christ is descended from David "according to the flesh" (as to his humanity)
  - (Romans 9:5) the Messiah, as a human being, belongs to the Jewish race
  - (1 Timothy 3:16) Christ was manifested in the flesh
- Human Relationships and Standards - the word *sarx* is used to express human, natural relationships, conditions, and circumstances
  - (Romans 4:1) Abraham is our racial ancestor ("our forefather according to the flesh")
  - (Romans 9:3) The Israelites are my kinsmen ("according to the flesh"); (Romans 11:14) the Israelites are "my flesh"
  - (1 Corinthians 1:26) Paul says that not many believers are wise, nobly born, and so forth, by human standards ("according to the flesh")

- ○ (1 Corinthians 7:28) Paul warns married people that they will have trouble ("in the flesh"), that is, in their natural relationship as husbands and wives
- ○ (1 Corinthians 9:11; Romans 15:27) Paul contrasts material benefits (*sarkika*) with spiritual benefits
- ○ (Galatians 3:3) Paul tells his readers that their Christian life began "in the spirit" but that now they were trying to complete it "in the flesh"
- Mortal Man - *Sarx* is used to describe man as weak, frail, mortal, and inadequate. In this word usage, which arises naturally from other noticed usage, "flesh" becomes associated with sin.
  - ○ (Romans 8:3) Paul speaks of what the Law of Moses could not do because it was weak "through the flesh"
  - ○ (Romans 7) Paul has a long discussion on the relation between the Law of Moses and sin
  - ○ Various passages that Paul warns believers against the influence of the "flesh" (Romans 13:14; Galatians 5:!3; Colossians 2:23)

Looking into the details of the usage of "flesh" in the Bible gives us a good level of understanding that it is beyond just the synonym for sexual lust. It is indeed the fallen human nature that controls nonbelievers, as well as, temptation that seeks to control believers. The usage and some of its attachment to historical aspects somehow give us a wider perspective of this word and find our way to relate in our current lives. The passages indicating Christ's humanity established a good portion of the foundation of our beliefs that He existed in human form but was not sinful. And every attempt of evil to deceive our thoughts on Jesus' display of anger in Matthew 21:12-17, is not an excuse for us, humans, to mingle ourselves in His righteous anger. Rather, may it serve as a constant reminder of His authority in us and the unrighteousness of this world. To further keep ourselves from being confused about this truth and understanding how flesh falls into the temptation of sin, we can check the famous story of Adam and Eve.

Before the serpent's appearance, the first couple was focused on God's authority - His design, will, and purpose for them. Once the serpent appeared and communicated, Eve's desire changed. It led to the (1) appetite for food, which brushed off God's command, and (2) being wise (Genesis 3:6). Followed by Adam, in his weak and frail flesh, changed allegiance from being directed to God's authority to "one another" with Eve. From this incident, we noticed how God's authority was displaced by the self-authority and vulnerability that Satan and the world influenced. Indeed the operations of flesh are impacted by desire. This desire becomes sinful when the focus removes God and His authority. Stirring up the sinful desire has been the evil's basic tactic, and his craftiness leads us to temptation. Funny how our shallowness is directly equating flesh to lust, considering there's no "third party" in the fall of Adam and Eve to the evil scheme. [19] Mr. Tarrants noted;

> *"Over the centuries, the church has gained deep insight into the flesh and the main sins that characterized it. These insights have been organized and refined into a schema now known as the seven deadly sins: pride, envy, anger, gluttony, lust, greed, and sloth."*

---

[19] Tarrants, T. III (2012). Hindrances to Discipleship. *C.S. Lewis Institute.* https://www.cslewisinstitute.org/

We can see the relativeness of these seven deadly sins in the words of Paul to the church of Galatians;

> *"Now the deeds of the flesh are evident, which are: immorality, impurity, sensuality, idolatry, sorcery, enmities, strife, jealousy, outbursts of anger, disputes dissensions, factions, envying, drunkenness, carousing, and things like these, of which I forewarn you, just as I have forewarned you, that those who practice such things will not inherit the kingdom of God." (Galatians 5:19-21, NASB1995)*

Annie and I (Rey) surely have a long list of instances in which we fell prey to the temptation of the flesh, yet the most profound experience is discovering the evil's craftiness in my life circumstances from a broken family. This may sound like a deep haul of the past, but my observation on how I've used anger or temper as a "protection shield" (which I mentioned in Chapter 1) was from disappointments, frustrations, and pain collected during the critical season of my parent's separation. I thought I had learned to move forward and the healing process was done, not knowing the collected pain had established a system and behavior leading to sinful responses of anger or temper. I had a simple desire to have my own family and not let my children experience a painful tragedy similar to my parents' separation. But since this desire was initiated during the season that I was not in a relationship with God and grounded in His words, the "enemy" was crafty enough to turn such noble desire into self-centeredness.

My (Rey) silence was not always translated to accepting matters surrounding me. Sometimes, it is in an attempt of my expression to control anger and outbursts of frustration. So, when my past two marriages showed evidence that it would be another challenging situation for me, my action on moving forward may not have an episode of outburst of anger but rather silence with immediate divorce paper. I accepted the financial burden that left me with those two divorces and thought those were enough "payment" for my sin of broken marriages. I tried to move forward, believing I would still have my own family. When I met Annie, my desire to have my family somewhat brightened. The need to discuss my past marriages somehow created a certain level of understanding, and our common desire contributed to solidifying our initial foundation. The effect of my broken relationship with my father was not put into deeper understanding rather, I relied on the comfort of isolating him. It was easy, I'm here in the US and he was there in the Philippines. I never knew how much anger I had in my heart until things in my growing family became complicated because of challenges. My long absence from them during periods of deployments weren't helpful at all. Just when we moved here to Las Vegas last 2011, which marked our 4 years in marriage, that allowed me to have a full circle with my family. Until the day arrived when I took action in God's call and marked my initial healing process - forgiveness to my father.

When I (Annie) met Rey, my impression of men with multiple divorces changed. It's a common perception of a man, who's divorced, of being a womanizer. Yet in his case, I found a good man with a sincere desire to have a family that he's been longing for since a young age. It seems that things didn't work out. However, I had a sense of understanding from hearing his side but the reality of his participation in the relationship came to life when it was my turn to be his wife. Things changed a lot when we moved here to the US and we started to experience the financial burden that was left on him from those first two past marriages. Our plan of lighting up such a load with me working was put on hold when we started to have more kids. Aside from such, I got a real deal of what it's like to be a military wife - who is often left at home and requires a unique independence. The first two years were fine because he was not on the ship, but his transfer to ship duty added more stretch to our marriage. Our adjustment was calculated. Not just in moving places and adjusting to a community that we're stationed in but also in our relationship as things get complicated. He'll be away for 6 months of deployment and stay home but still with training that will require him to be away for a couple of days (even a week). We can discuss things but the boundaries were evident, particularly in matters of his work. There are things that he can't share with me and I will notice how more silent he was in the first week of his arrival from deployment. I felt so alone in a marriage that was continuously sailing. In times that I have to raise concerns there's an evident anger. I wish I could tell I've responded well to all those moments but many times I failed to do so and I've triggered more of such anger. I'm so thankful that God saved us. It was just in that moment that I witnessed Rey's different vulnerability. I never realized the load of pain he has in his heart until God softened it and revealed what's been deeply occupying his inner self.

We often ignore and give less attention to the level of degree that the weakness of flesh has brought on us. Whether we're exposed to God's words or not, the common response to weakness is to either ignore or find a way to lessen or avoid the attention. The reality of brokenness is leading us to passiveness until God stirs up our hearts and orchestrates situations so we can have that opportunity to grow in humility as we face the reality of our weaknesses. Only then we be on the clear path of repentance which is only possible when we have that genuine humility that reconciles and units with God through Jesus Christ. In [20]Dr. Jerry Root's series for "The Screwtape Letters" in CS Lewis Institute, he mentioned in the episode of "Sins of the Flesh;"

> *"All of us are broken. Well, let me put it this way. All of us are wounded and brokenness I think is the awareness of our wounds and how it affects us on some level."*

Instead of surrendering those wounds to Christ and embracing His blessings of discipleship, we keep ignoring Him. Even in the effort of understanding such, we're disconnecting it from Jesus Christ, who has full knowledge of our hearts and understands the pain that we've been through (or going through). We have to stop viewing flesh from different perspectives far from God's truth. Continue living in shallowness by thinking that "feeling good" is the answer to the reality of our weakness. We can rely on Christ to face the reality of life. Jesus Christ didn't come to simply help us to feel good in this life. He came to help us to be good. Our God is more concerned with our holiness than our happiness. [21] Mr. Tarrants said;

> *"If we ever hope to make progress as disciples of Jesus - to think as He thought, to want what He wants, to feel as He felt, to act as He acted - we must understand and deal*

---

[20] Root, J. (2010, October 4). *The Screwtape Letters: Sins of flesh*. C.S. Lewis Institute. https://www.cslewisinstitute.org/

[21] Tarrants, T. III (2012). Hindrances to Discipleship. *C.S. Lewis Institute.* https://www.cslewisinstitute.org/

with our flesh and the sins it produces. This means being ruthlessly honest with ourselves about ourselves in the light of God's Word and Spirit and then putting to death the sinful works of the flesh through the power of the Holy Spirit. As we do so, we will grow in the grace and knowledge and likeness of Jesus and glorify God more and more. We will discover that a holy life is a happy life. "

Hindrances to Discipleship: The Evil

Even in the effort to organize the collective wisdom to understand the true meaning and distinctions of the hindrances in following Christ (which is also in discipleship), there's an obvious interrelation and evident participation of evil. The "world" where we get a chance to experience God's blessings of life, has remained in noticeable exitance of the evil that surrounds us with temptation and evil schemes waiting for us to fall prey. Our "flesh" which serves as the temple of the Holy Spirit (1 Corinthians 6:19-20), requires a consistent spiritual discipline so our weaknesses will not be Satan's object for his continuous nefarious works. The reasons are obvious that we need to stop avoiding and continue journeying this life with ignorance of Satan.

"Every era has had its own blind spots, and ours is no exception. A notable example in our day is the denial of the existence of the Devil. " [22] (Mr. Thomas Tarrants III)

Despite the blessings of available resources nowadays, even the Bible itself, we don't give time to articulate ourselves on who truly Satan is, his character, his works,

---

[22] Tarrants, T. III (2012). Hindrances to Discipleship. *C.S. Lewis Institute.* https://www.cslewisinstitute.org/

and his objectives. Our wrong perceptions and ignorance have led us to be unconsciously attached to him. We don't have a good and full understanding of its impact on ourselves as well as in our marriage. In reality, the devil has considerable power to create harm in pursuing evil goals even though he doesn't have absolute control over the world. This doesn't mean that we'll ignore and limit our understanding, but rather we should establish a good level of awareness so we'll be continuously encouraged and focused to rely on God and the mighty power of the Holy Spirit.

> *"For our struggle is not against flesh and blood, but against the rulers, against the powers, against the world forces of this darkness, against the spiritual forces of wickedness in the heavenly places."* (Ephesians 6:12, NASB1995)

We were commanded to be alert (1 Peter 5:8), encouraged to be strong in the Lord, and put on the full armor of God (Ephesians 6:11-12). In the first place if we're not aware of the "object" to be alert, the one that leads us to vulnerability and shakes our sanctification process, then we're setting ourselves to moral blindness. Satan may have various approaches but he normally tempts us to sin. Such sin will continue to stay lost on those who are already lost or delay sanctification and breakthroughs to those who are exposed to God's truths. So discover the object or reasons that trigger you to fall into the temptation's trap, and understand why and how it triggers you. Then seek God's help and rely on the Holy Spirit to work earnestly. From the beginning of the process until reaching that significant breakthrough remain in God, because Satan's goal of sin affects our relationship and submission to God and His authority. We shared more details of Satan in the next chapter, *"Reality of Spiritual Warfare."*

CHAPTER 5
REALITY OF SPIRITUAL WARFARE

There's an undeniable recognition of the significance and importance of discipleship in our Christian walk. It surely did affect our marriage and other relationships. The feeling of gratefulness will always be there especially when we recollect testimonies that we never thought would be possible for both of us. Yet there's also conviction calling for humility that provides awareness of where we might be apart from Him. This part of awareness also drives us to the areas where we're having difficulties navigating and are often tempted. These are the open manholes on our journey which are constantly active and could strongly sack us in. Thus, giving us challenges to get up and move forward. Indeed they are speedbumps in our journey.

For instance, our initial attendance at a couple's seminar stood as the beginning of the numerous couples' retreats and faith-based conferences that we attended. Despite our sincere willingness to learn as well as our open heart for accountability, we still find ourselves amid conflicts. Sometimes the conflict started from a very simple situation that could have been prevented if we remembered our lesson in communication or submission. Submission is not just in the context of wife to husband, but also our submission, as a united married couple, to God's call on a particular situation or incident. Another side is our responses when disagreement or conflict arises. We all know that conflict is inevitable and will certainly take place in this broken "world", but our deliverance in every conflict is heavily dependent on our responses. We know that this is another area in us that we need improvement.

If we look at these numerous incidents or the areas that require our improvement, we will surely be discouraged. It's only by God's grace that we remained to stay on track with our journey, and reached this point of sharing our experience through this book. So when God impressed on us with the concept of this book, we knew that we needed to include the discussion about "spiritual warfare." This doesn't mean that our confidence and openness to this topic automatically equates that we're an expert on it. Today, we're still learning and growing in this area. So, our sharing of experience relating to this covers the discovery and realization of its reality, experiences, and how we view it as we move forward.

"Spiritual Warfare" has nothing to do with physical battles. The name itself gives a clear understanding that it's the battle in spirit. It is the inward and outward battle we have to face as followers of Christ against God's enemies or any temptation that could let us fall into like lust of the eyes, the lust of the flesh, and the danger of pride. As we continue in this Christianity journey, and we learn God's holiness, we'll observe and recognize that battle forming from our internal spirit and the sinful nature of our flesh. For example in the context of marriage, as we learn God's design of this relationship and our relationships, we'll have this desire and conviction to follow God and His perspective in this relationship. Yet, our natural sinful flesh could lead us to moral blindness which further delays our potential progression in obeying God. In this battle, we need to learn how to let ourselves recognize the power of the Holy Spirit, and continuously grow with it.

Why spiritual warfare is difficult to recognize or often neglected?

Sadly, there is a noticeable discomfort or avoidance in discussions about Spiritual Warfare because of its direct message about the reality of Satan's existence. It's not a regular subject of many group discussions - small or big, particularly between husband and wife. Imagine the objections to just accepting the truth that we're all sinners. How much more in the reality that Satan exists, actively deceiving and influencing us! Imagine a wife telling her husband (or vice versa), "You're being influenced again by Satan!" In the Philippines' local language, "*dinidemonyo ka na naman!*" Many may have used this line in humor but in critical situations, this will surely be chaos. The challenge of accepting and navigating the truth of Satan's existence and having influence may automatically result in rejection and further division in the relationship. Our journey in learning more about this was not easy. It's a continuous learning process even today, and we're thankful to God for His grace as we experience His comfort and guidance in between. Every time we're caught in circumstances that test our awareness and responses to spiritual warfare, we're learning to hold tighter to God. Truly, this is not something that we could easily learn by reading alone. It's heavily experiential and allows us to exercise the message of Salvation. In times that this matter will be included in our regular sharing time, it made us think about why there's an evident struggle in learning about spiritual warfare, acknowledging its reality, and the need to not neglect it.

Over the years of our intentional journey in Christianity, our experiences have led us to understand the common reasons why we're having difficulty recognizing or giving importance to not neglecting spiritual warfare. Surely, there are many other reasons or factors, but with our experiences, we concluded that these three factors took major space.

Reason 1: We're not used to the reality of the spiritual realm

It's not a natural thing for us (humans) to recognize and get used to these spiritual realms like spiritual warfare, the power of the Holy Spirit, and the experiential reality of God's existence. Our separation from God has led us to the innocence of these truths and how significant they are in our lives today. It's a blessing if we grow up in a household that's intentional in establishing the foundation of our identity anchored in God. Yet, still, when we reach a certain age and need to start living on our own, that guidance, particularly concerning the spiritual realm, will be tested on how well we understand it and determine its relevance and significance in our life today. Genesis 2:7 has an important word that defines God's creation and design for us as not just physical;

> *"Then the Lord formed a man of dust from the ground, and breathed into his nostrils the breath of life, and man became a living being."* (Genesis 2:7, NASB 1995)

The word "being" in the phrase "living being" is from the Hebrew word [23]"lenefesh"(lə·ne·p̄eš), which means a soul, living being, life, self, person. We're created as a living soul - not only capable of performing functions similar to animal life such as eating, drinking, and walking but we have thinking, reasoning, and discoursing as a rational creature.

---

[23] Strong's Concordance, www.biblehub.com

Another verse that clearly defines God's creation for us is in the writings of the Apostle Paul;

> *"Now may the God of peace Himself sanctify you entirely; and may your spirit and soul and body be preserved complete, without blame at the coming of our Lord Jesus Christ."* (1 Thessalonians 5:23, NASB1995)

A prayer that we may be sanctified and press toward this holiness not just in our physical body but also in spirit and soul. An apostle's petition that we will be blameless until the coming of Jesus Christ. Our good understanding of our being and God's design for us don't just let us view life here in this world but with the great importance of our spirit and soul.

[24]C.S. Lewis mentioned in *"The Screwtape Letters"* that as humans we're amphibious creatures. We are both spiritual and embodied. Embodied souls. Lewis says that our soul has at least three components;

1. Thinking that features reason
2. Feeling that features emotion
3. Choosing that features volition (one's will)

These three components show how God differentiates us from animals and have these components stand as another way to be connected with Him. In [25]Dr. Jerry Root broadcast talk for C.S. Lewis Institute entitled "Spiritual Warfare in a Material World, " he noted how "reason" is the weakest of those three;

---

[24] Lewis, C.S. (2012). The Screwtape Letters. William Collins

[25] Dr. Jerry Root, "Spiritual Warfare in a Material World" (Broadcast Talk, CS Lewis institute, Volume 8 Number 4, 2023)

"I want to suggest to you - even coming from an academic environment - the reason is hands down, the weakest of those three. If I make a stupid choice with my volition, my will, my reason doesn't kick in and say, "Boy, Jerry, you made a stupid decision. If you continue down the line, you're just going to hurt yourself, and you're going to hurt others. You need to repent of that and get back on track."
No, my reason, being weak, is marshaled by my volition to make all kinds of excuses and rationalizations for that bad choice. It keeps me in a state of moral blindness."

The reality is, that these three components will be Satan's venue to conduct decisiveness leading to spiritual warfare. So not until we allow ourselves to learn about this spiritual realm, experience the reality of God, and the power of the Holy Spirit, we will always get lost in the battle of spiritual warfare.

Just like Dr. Root, our weak point is "reason". Remember the list of 5 challenges that we shared in Chapter 1? Those sins that we declared when we accepted Jesus Christ and claimed His forgiveness. Well, those are the objects that Satan continues to pursue, tempt us, interrupt our repentance, wiggle the sanctification process, and even put blurriness in God's purpose for us and our marriage. On the other hand, those could also be the very things God uses to lead us to Him and be closer to Him. In these two potential scenarios, we can surely determine the active role of spiritual warfare. Just like [26]Dr. Root further note in this matter;

---

[26] Dr. Jerry Root, *"Spiritual Warfare in a Material World"* I(Broadcast Talk, CS Lewis institute, Volume 8 Number 4, 2023)

"The whole issue of our Christian life is the sanctification process of restoring the image of Christ; consequently, that's going to factor into spiritual warfare."

Our ignorance of the "spiritual realm" also extends to not fully understanding the "sanctification process," which is very significant in our journey and this spiritual warfare. To sanctify a certain object means to clean, consecrate, or set aside for a special purpose. Sanctification is Christian teachings about God's transformation into a person, being fit for a holy purpose. It includes a change of heart, a change of mind, and embracing God's truth [27]. This isn't overtime. We don't immediately become loving, kind, humble, and self-controlled. There's a growing or progression stage just like a child turning into an adult (1 Peter 2:2). Our ignorance on this, leads us to not recognize God's work in us and the spiritual battle is becoming tougher.

Reason 2: We've become "materialistic"

Although the Bible kept a good record that will lead us to a good understanding of Spiritual Warfare, yet we end up with the common impression that this exists in the form of exorcism only. This leads us to a certain level of fear to even look into it, take time to understand it, and discover its significance in our current lives.

In a similar talk, [28] Dr. Jerry Root noted that Satan is real and busy gearing the traffic of our fear.

---

[27] Cru Ministry, "What is Sanctification and How Does it Work?, www.cru.org

[28] Dr. Jerry Root, *"Spiritual Warfare in a Material World"* (Broadcast Talk, CS Lewis institute, Volume 8 Number 4, 2023)

And if we don't hold on to the truth and experience the reality that perfect love casts out fear (1 John 4:18), we will always find ourselves lost in Satan's traffic of fear. When we heard about this, we reflected on the story of Adam and Eve with the serpent's influence on that forbidden fruit. This story impacted us on how Satan works and the magnitude of the responses from Adam and Eve. Since day one, we have seen how Satan hates unity and living for God's purpose. It was just a series of questions that initiated the doubts and triggered a different desire for Eve to take that bite and pass on the fruit to Adam.

Today, the "forbidden fruit" has come a long way. It could be some big and obvious tragedy that directly affects the couple's trust in each other like adultery, or simple things we often avoid and just give little attention such as being annoyed by delayed text messaging. There's a great difference in the magnitude but both come with a certain degree of danger and significant impact to marriage. Sometimes those consistent little habits are the ones that will bring callousness in the relationship and build walls of pride, envy, greed, jealousy, hatred, and more.

We tend to equate most life aspects like love, care, and others, with tangible things and measurable factors. Just like how we measure our spouse's devotion to marriage and family; by evaluating the contribution within the parameters of time, effort, and even money, alone. Sadly, the same goes when we think of God and His blessings. We're quick to view Him through our life circumstances and we're so comforted by the thought that His blessings always come with material things or any tangible factors that are directly providing comfort in our lives.

Reason 3: Our ignorance of Satan's character and works

Our life separated from God doesn't just put blindness in the spiritual realm or turn us materialistic, but it lets us be in a certain degree of ignorance of Satan's character and active works in today's life.

Because it is seldom that we give attention to this character, we lose the reality that he exists in this world. Our minds were settled on the thought of his existence during the incident in the garden with Adam and Eve. After that, we lost awareness of what he's still doing today, particularly towards marriage and family. Sadly, we will only take action when we catch ourselves entangled in his tactics and we're facing the reality and impact of consequences.

In one of [29]The New Inductive Study Series of Kay Arthur and Pete De Lacy, (study of the book of Job) "Trusting God in Times of Adversity" they noted;

> *"The word Satan means adversary. As in a way, learning in advance all you can about opponents can help you know how they operate and what offensive and defensive countermeasures to make to gain advantages. By the time the New Testament authors composed their writings, the church had a great deal of Biblical information about the devil. Paul could say that we're not ignorant of his tactics."* (2 Corinthians 2:11)."

So to eliminate the idea that Satan is only God's adversary, we can learn from the life of Job how Satan becomes his adversary. From this, we can see clear similarities and relevance in our lives today. As we reflect

---

[29] Arthur, K. & De Lacy, P. (2003). The New Inductive Study Series, Job: "Trusting God in Times of Adversity". Harvest House Publishers

on Job 1, we can learn about Satan - his character, tactics, and the limits God places on his power.

Learnings about Satan

1. Satan can be in a group with believers.

We have this impression that Satan won't be or even close near to a group of believers. So our effort of having our spouse nor our entire family be devoted to God will keep us away and safe from Satan doesn't even go near to the reality of where Satan stays or mingles.

> *"Now there was a day when the sons of God, came to present themselves before the Lord, and Satan also came among them."* (Job 1:6, NASB1995)

The sons of God came to present themselves to give an account of what they had observed and done, and Satan also came among them. Two common things that this verse is taken out of context and puts blurriness in connection to our current lives are; (1) the council of God is literally angels only or just a group in a "church" context, and (2) Satan is a physical form being and can visually recognize today. The phrase "sons of God" doesn't just only apply to the context of angels nor the body of the church as an organization. Jesus Christ, the Son of God, made it clear in Matthew 18:20 that when two or three gathered together in His name, He was there in the midst (Ecclesia). The body or collective "sons of God" is not being measured by numerical standards but by its fulfillment of the true conditions of its life.

Secondly, we just assume that Satan is evil in physical form. [30]The Bible doesn't tell us exactly what Satan looks like in terms of physical appearance. Although the Bible does tell us that at times he can be assumed to be in physical form, such as when Satan tempted Jesus to turn away from God in Matthew 4:1-11.

So, to better understand Satan's participation in today's gathering or group of 2 to 3 believers, we can refer to Satan's action through the meaning of his name. [31]The word rendered "Satan" is derived from שׂטן śaṭan "*Satan*," to lie in wait (conceal oneself, waiting to surprise, attack or catch someone), to be an adversary, and hence, it means properly an adversary, an accuser.

In between the two of us (Rey & Annie), we found ourselves in numerous instances of putting so much light on each other's weaknesses and the effect of past brokenness that we carried and let affect the supposed path of complete deliverance. Little that we know we've been Satan's object. Upon discovering this, we intentionally discussed our behavior and analyzed our responses, not to accuse each other but to determine the patterns and what drives or triggers those behaviors. We're also able to determine how we affect each other with our behavior and responses. Such action alone is God's blessing to start releasing ourselves of Satan's hook and pave the way to learn - take actions with a more understanding approach.

Speaking of Satan's temptation to Jesus Christ (Matthew 4:1-11), we can check on Jesus' experience with Satan while He's living here on earth. Jesus called Satan the father of lies (John 8:44). In 2 Corinthians 11:14, Satan disguises himself as an angel of light.

---

[30] Q&A, Billy Graham Evangelistic Association of Canada, www.billygraham.ca

[31] Job 1:6 Commentary. Barnes' Notes on the Bible. Bible Hub, www.biblehub.com

The allusion may be because of his appearance along with "sons of God" in Job's story, nevertheless, he twists scripture in Matthew 4:5-6, the temptation of Christ in the wilderness. Satan uses scripture to tempt Jesus Christ. He is a scripture twister.

When I (Rey) started reading the Bible, I learned a lot of God's wonderful works, and I realized how Annie and I have been Satan's objects in lies and twisted truths in our past lives. We make narrations that are far from the truth as long as it will be beneficial for our selfish desires. Since the discovery that Satan is the father of lies, we've committed ourselves not to be his object in this matter and we tried to extend such learnings to our children. I always remind our children, how their mom and I suffered for the twisted truths and now that we commit ourselves to Christ, it will be part of our household's core values not to lie. Even if it hurts, don't lie because once this catches you, Satan will continue to cripple you and will proceed with his work until damages happen.

My (Rey's) collection of learnings and discoveries of God's recorded works in the Bible have sparked a desire in my heart to experience Him. So when I come across in Malachi 3:10, the Lord said, "Test me in this," my prayer was not to question His power but to personally experience His power. Some other parts in the Bible that we can check on God's encouragement to man (to us) for testing are Isaiah 7:10-14 and 1 John 4:1. Some may think that this is confusing on Jesus' statement in Matthew 4.7. The meaning here is not to test God by throwing ourselves voluntarily and in uncommanded dangers, then appeal to God for protection. God indeed helps us, who also allows trials, but it's not true that the promise extends to those who deliberately provoke

Him and trifle with the promised help. As [32]C.H. Spurgeon commented;

> *"I know some people, who earn their living in employments which are very hazardous to their immortal souls. They are in the midst of evil, yet they tell me that God can keep them in safety there. I know that he can, but I also know that we have no right to go, voluntarily, where we are surrounded by temptation. If your calling is the wrong one, and you are continually tempted by it, you may not presume upon the goodness of God to keep you, for it is your business to get as far as you can from that which will lead you into sin. God does not put his servants on the pinnacle of the temple; it is the devil who puts them there; and if they ever are there, the best thing they can do is to get down as quickly and as safely as they can; but they must not cast themselves down, they must look to him who alone can bring them down safely. With some professors, presumption is a very common sin. They will go into worldly amusements and all sorts of frivolities, and say, "Oh, we can be Christians, and yet go there!" Can you? It may be that you can be hypocrites, and go there; that is far easier than going there as Christians."*

Here we can see how Satan creatively twists the Scriptures, which is supposedly the basis and foundation of believers' communication and way of life.

    2. Satan continuously searches the world, never passing, never resting.

---

[32] Spurgeon's Verse Exposition of the Bible. Truth According to the Scriptures. www.truthaccordingtoscripture.com

"The Lord said to Satan, 'From where do you come?' Then Satan answered the Lord and said, 'From roaming about on the earth and walking around it.'" (Job 1:7, NASB1995)

The questioning of God in this verse could make us confused as there's a truth that God knows everything (1 John 3:20, Psalm 147:5). The questioning is not for God's addition to His knowledge but for the "sons of God", who were present, might hear and call their attention to the doings of Satan. These doings would need to be watched and sometimes to be restrained or (can be) prevented. That's why we're reminded to guard our hearts (Proverbs 4:23) and warn our fellow believers (Matthew 18:15-20; Ezekiel 3:18-19). With God's question and Satan's answer, it's clear that Satan searches the whole earth continually, never passing, never resting like a roaring lion seeking someone to devour (1 Peter 5:8). This reminds us that there could be instances where God will intentionally stir-up conversation so Satan will be heard by believers, then realization and awareness of his existence will take place. Thus, we should remind ourselves not to be too comfortable nor to be anxious, but just be alert.

This is one of those many things that caught us by surprise and learned the hard way. We'll talk more in the next chapter about how our ignorance of Satan's voice and neglecting it affected ourselves, our marital relationship, and even our relationship with others.

3. Satan notices God's servant (even God's genuine servants don't escape Satan's tricks)

"The Lord said to Satan, 'Have you considered My servant Job? For there is no one like him on the earth, a blameless

and upright man, fearing God and turning away from evil." (Job 1:8, NASB1995)

It's one of the common wrong perceptions that being a "servant of God" is having a position that flows within the four corners of a church building. Learning Job's life provides a clear understanding that a servant of God is not just in the context of "church position" but extends even to the simplest status in life. Job 1 & 2 shows us that;

- Job is blameless, upright, fearing God, and turning away from evil (Job 1:1)
- Job has sons and daughters (Job 1:2) and his faithfulness to God extends to making sacrifices for the thought that his sons may have sinned (Job 1:5)
- Job has possessions - a good estate to support his family, considered as wealthy at that time (Job 1:3) and evidently blessed in the work of his hands (Job 1:10)
- Job has servants (Job 1:14-15)
- Job holds fast to his integrity (Job 2:3)
- Job has a wife (Job 2:9)

Relating the description of Job's life to today's generation, we can conclude that he is a married man with children, successful (wealthy), and faithfully walking in God. This just reminds us that being God's servant goes beyond the church's position. It may include even if you're a family man or a stay-at-home mother.

God's question to Satan for consideration of testing Job, tells us that (1) no one escapes Satan's tricks, and (2) Satan will only have the power to test us when approved by God. It's not to put fear in us and to be discouraged in faithfully serving God for whatever status we have, but it's a reminder of God's power. It's not for our breakage but for us to learn and experience how to be truly dependent on Him.

4.   Satan promotes selfishness.

"Then Satan answered the Lord, 'Does Job fear God for nothing?" (Job 1:9, NASB1995)

Satan, the "accuser", boldly and quickly accuses Job of his righteousness and faithful walk in God as self-serving (to keep the blessings). Satan's statement denotes that Job serves God, not for the love of God or love of goodness, but for what he gets (blessings and protection).

Truly, it's not easy to be in the position to be questioned and be doubted on the services that we're doing for God. This just doesn't flow inside the context of "church service" but our love for God that's interpreted in how we do our work/business, raising our children, and the bold changes that we're doing in our lives. In times like this, we're reminding ourselves that God is just, and He will always treat us fairly. He knows our circumstances, our motives, and our hearts, so His decisions are always based on absolute truth, as found in Deuteronomy 32:4. And in times that neither one of us is tempted on Satan's trick to be selfish, we're tightly holding one's hands, embracing God's grace and mercy, and intentionally supporting each other towards repentance.

5.   Satan is under the Lord's power to test the Saint's faithfulness.

"Then the Lord said to Satan, 'Behold all that he has is in your power, only do not put forth your hand on him,' So Satan departed from the presence of the Lord." (Job 1:12)

Satan receives permission to test Job, but there's an evident limitation, "do not put forth your hand on him." God allowed him to do it. We may be wondering why God should give Satan such permission. He did it for His glory, to honor Job, to understand providence (that God cares for and provides for people's lives and His involvement in how things go), and to encourage His afflicted people of all ages. Just like us today, we're encouraged by Job's story and hold on to what God has done to him when we're undergoing challenges. God let Job, a family man, suffer, to be tested just like He suffered Peter, a disciple, to be sifted but took care that his faith should not fail (Luke 22:31-32). Such trials and sufferings were directed and ended for praise, honor, and glory to God (1 Peter 1:7).

However, let's not forget that God has Satan in chain (Revelations 20:1-2). Satan could not test Job without God's permission, and similar goes for us today. We are under God's protection and nothing can snatch us away from Him even Satan (Romans 8:31-39).

Satan is real. Spiritual warfare comes in as Satan continues to oppose God's works and deprive the glory that's due to Him. Satan desires to keep the lost people to remain lost. As well as to deceive those who found the truth and go back to being lost. The great deal is our responses, as it will show how deeply rooted God's truth is in our hearts. So, if you still haven't committed yourself to Christ, will you remain lost in His truth and be Satan's object? Or you have already declared, yet continue to set boundaries and not fully surrender, thus letting yourself be an easy object of Satan's deceiveness? In both of these questions, you will determine our (Rey & Annie) guilt as our shortcomings following these questions are recognizable in the stories we mentioned. It's only God's grace that He opened our eyes to the reality of "spiritual warfare," and how we should remain accountable to our responses. It is indeed a continuous process and it's not by any physical means or capability. It's our continuous inclination to the power and influence of the Holy Spirit.

Whether we're facing hardships in life or we're able to keep things working out, anticipating that the sacrifices in coming to Christ will make us more miserable or miss the fun in this life - that's wrong! We used to believe that we could live this life within the reach of our wisdom, skills, and resources. Little that we know that there's more in this life. The journey to deliverance and undergoing the sanctification process may come with some roughness, particularly the consideration of spiritual warfare. Yet in the end, God is faithful to remind us that the best decision we've made is choosing and following Jesus Christ. So in every moment that we find ourselves and our marriage facing a spiritual battle, it's God's way to remind and train us to strengthen our connection with Him - through the power of the Holy Spirit.

CHAPTER 6
REDEFINING MOMENT

It is indeed foundational to our Christian walk to understand Satan's tricks and limits of the power that God places on him. The knowledge of Satan's existence leads us to a better understanding of spiritual warfare. Thank God for today's technology. The blessing of today's great authors, speakers, and testimony sharers is just at our fingertips. Although our personal commitment and consistent engagement to God's words remain the best source in understanding our (1) own lives, (2) the vulnerability we're experiencing because of the sins we committed, and (3) the significant impact of God's grace, mercy, and love. Thus, it drives us to continue navigating this life anchored in Him and His words. Like other sharers and God's witnesses, our eagerness to learn and experience Him didn't just stay within the boundaries of discovering His truths through reading and fellowshipping with other believers. God assured us that we will have a personal experience of the reality of His words and the calling to be His servants - to be His Son's disciples and followers.

As mentioned in Chapter 4, I (Rey) tried to be a responsible provider in our family by looking for a job to help with our financial difficulties. At that time, the business was still fairly running, and God allowed me to experience His provision as I took night shifts in driving services around Las Vegas. Since there wasn't a significant progression in our financial status, I thought securing a job would make a difference. Little did I know that God's revelation on my answered prayers, when I asked for earnings in my driving services, was a clear message that all help comes from Him alone (Psalm 121:2). I experienced difficulties in getting a job, but I remained faithful and hopeful. When the day arrived, I received a favorable response to one of my job applications. The complications in schedule and other factors that we intend to keep as we commit ourselves to living a new life under His authority made me realize whether this job opening was God's blessing or Satan's way to lose track of faithfully living under His authority. I consulted a fellow believer whose comment on my dilemma raised further doubts. He said, *"Go, get the job, and don't tell Annie."* Although I respect this man, his comment conflicts with God's design for a couple's unity. It is doubtful and different from what we commonly hear from our other trusted friends and fellow believers. They will usually encourage us to have a discussion, ask God for help, and surrender the decision to God. For that week, I eagerly sought direction from God through His words and constant prayer. My reading habit comes in two ways. I started reading the Bible from beginning to end and remained on that cycle even today. I also follow the YouVersion's "Verse of the Day" but read the whole chapter instead of just the scheduled verse or verses. On that particular week, God's message was consistent, "Come and serve Me." Surprisingly, in both ways of my Bible reading, His message was the same.

On the other hand, I (Annie) was bothered when Rey started looking for a new job. We were already finding difficulties navigating the business, his nights out on the road, and keeping on the ministry schedule. When I look at our situation, we're somehow adapting to this "Christian life," and my heart is screaming, *"God, we're obeying You now, but why we're still in this situation?"* Rey may also have the same question; that's why he's trying to find a new job. Our constant engagement in the small group reminds me of my role as a wife - to submit to my husband. My desire to obey God through submission stopped my objection to questioning Rey for his decision. However, I continued asking God for peace and guidance so that Rey could be equipped with his decision. I didn't know that I was already amid spiritual warfare. When the day arrived, I realized I was anxious between my morning quiet time, constant meditation on God's words, and listening to Biblical teachings. I'm anxious about losing help in the business we planned to redeem. I'm anxious that Rey will lose track of our intentional journey to Christianity. I'm anxious that this new job will affect our ministry schedule and eventually cause us to lose our intentionality in our growing faith. Indeed, Satan's craftiness and creativity will draw our attention to the things that we thought were in obedience to God. Yet the truth is, Satan is playing in our hearts and minds, so we will be tempted to take matters into our own hands alone and not consult God. So I brought myself to my knees and asked God for deliverance on that anxiousness and to guide me in helping Rey.

The day finally arrived, and I (Rey) needed to decide on the job opening. God's message was clear, and I had to obey. God spoke to me in Jeremiah 15:19-21. In Chapter 4, I shared how this verse helped me to embrace discipleship.

[19] *This is how the Lord responds: "If you return to me, I will restore you so you can continue to serve me. If you speak good words rather than worthless ones, you will be my spokesman. You must influence them; do not let them influence you!*

²⁰ *They will fight against you like an attacking army, but I will make you as secure as a fortified wall of bronze. They will not conquer you, for I am with you to protect and rescue you. I, the Lord , have spoken!*

²¹ *Yes, I will certainly keep you safe from these wicked men. I will rescue you from their cruel hands.*" (Jeremiah 15:19-21, NLT)

I (Rey) was convicted of my recent actions not defining trust in God. My persistence to put matters in my own hands didn't stop me from the signs God was showing me. Many of my job applications didn't push through to the next step stage because of many incidents that hindered me from proceeding. One day, I woke up with a swollen ankle. I can't barely walk and have to cancel the interview schedule. It was not until this last one that God let me proceed, but the heaviness in my heart was finally answered through His words. Do I really trust Him? I suddenly felt tears in my eyes and reflected deeper in these verses from Jeremiah. My tears weren't just from the conviction but gratitude for His promise. Despite my weakness, His grace reminded me of His promised restoration and deliverance. After prayer, I immediately went to Annie and checked her personal quiet time with God.

When Rey approached me in the corner of our formal living room, I (Annie) was completing my journal entry for that day. He caught me smiling. I was surprised to see him crying, and I immediately apologized that my big smile was not inviting at that particular moment. I let him share his encounter with God, and as I listened, I could see some connections in our devotions. When it was my turn to share my devotions and how God encountered me on that day, I explained the reason for smiling. During that time, I followed the book, *"Streams in the Desert,"* Daily Devotional by L.B. Cowman. On that particular day, I was supposed to reflect on John 7:38. Without double checking, my initial reading fell on John 6:38. So I turned the pages and again without consciously checking, I was reading John 8:38. Then, I turned the pages again and make sure that I'm reading John 7:38. I told Rey, it was a day of "38s," and surprisingly all those verses where words from Jesus Christ. Instead of reflecting on one verse that day, I included the other two verses. God may have been trying to tell me something that's not in my regular schedule.

"(Jesus said) For I have come down from heaven, not to do My own will, but the will of Him who sent Me." (John 6:38, NASB1995)

Looking at the whole chapter of John 6, we'll better understand the background of Jesus' words. John 6 starts with the story of Him feeding the five thousand people (John 6:1-14), then it follows with Jesus walking on the water (John 6:15-25). Then Jesus started talking to people about the signs that He had shown (John 6:26-40). He encouraged the people to seek Him not because of the loaves they ate nor because it was the reason for them to consider God's works so they'd receive food. Seek and attend to God's works because they believe in Him and Him (Jesus) being sent by God. This does not mean that we are not making an effort to supply our needs like food, but that we are not to be anxious in such supplication, particularly since we're obeying God's work. The continued inquiry has reached the people's belief of the previously recorded experience of mana provision with Moses, and such experience should also happen considering Jesus' claim that God sent him. Jesus then clearly stated that He is the "bread of life," the One who provides life to those separated from God (John 6:32-35). The separation leads many to seek signs before believing in God and eventually turn their devotion to the object/person used by God like Moses. Although here in John 6, Jesus did not just emphasize the object of belief, but He made a clear claim that God sent him.

Just like in our case, Rey and I (Annie) may sincerely intend to improve our situation, but the challenge of navigating the spiritual realm and facing our consequences affected our focus to rely on the job or rehabilitation of the business as ways for restoration towards security. In many testimonies that we've heard, we anticipated that we'll experience similar things. Instead of seeking God's ways, we were highly influenced by the pattern of those who've experienced breakthroughs with God, particularly in the financial aspect, and my (Annie's) heart shifted from God's ways to man's ways. There's nothing wrong with being motivated by those stories and the blessings of shared practical applications. The psalmist encouraged us to declare God's glory and marvelous works (Psalm 96:3), but God intends to stay focused on seeking His ways, a similar message that Jesus pointed out in John 6:26-40. The psalmist shared in Psalm 86:11 that God's ways are anchored in His truth with an engaged and united heart on Him, thus recognizing God's authority. Instead of focusing alone on the efforts or actions taken by the testimony sharer (good works alone), we need to pay more attention to how their heart has been transformed by God, which has resulted in repentance - taking actions. Furthermore, we can view God's grace in sending Jesus Christ to help those people then (even for us today) and reassure them that He's there to do God's will (John 6:38). So in Jesus' statement, we're not just getting the great confidence of Jesus' role and influence in terms of His recorded experience as human, but also the amazing moral oneness with God, the Father.

> *"There is no schism between the Father and Son. A separate will in and of itself assigned to the Son is not inconceivable, nay, it is imperatively necessary to posit, or we should lose all distinctions whatever between the Father and Son, between God and Christ. But the very separateness of the wills gives the greater significance to their moral oneness.....Christ declares that the Divine commission of His humanity is the spontaneous and free, but perfect, coincidence of His will with the Father's. Christ's embodiment of the Father's will, and coordination with it, make all his attractiveness to the human soul."* [33] (Pulpit Commentary)

Indeed, our obedience to God's will follows the pattern of Jesus Christ. On that day, I (Annie) am reminded that my reconciliation with Christ is not just directly equated to bettering our situation but having a heart that obeys God's will. Thus, we follow the pattern of Jesus Christ (Christlikeness). Yet we all know how difficult it could be to determine God's will, especially when we're not used to doing such. The same hardship goes in the attempt to live this life following Christ's pattern. It requires denying ourselves (Luke 9:23). So even if we try our very best to navigate this life relying on the resources that this world offers, we will indeed reach a point of "emptiness" or "thirst."

---

[33] John 6:38. Pulpit Commentary. www.biblehub.com

There will be a great challenge of finding genuine peace and contentment because of this world's tribulation. The only resolution is to be in union with Someone who has already overcome it, and that's Jesus Christ (John 16:33). We may not have a "physical form" of Jesus Christ today. Still, He pointed out that our "thirst" - the strong desire for His presence will come in spiritual form, which He noted in John 7:38.

> "(*Jesus said) He who believes in Me, as the Scripture said, 'From his innermost being will flow rivers of living water."* (John 7:38, NASB1995)

God's declaration of promises written in the Scripture indicates that our submission to Jesus' authority comes with the blessing of the satisfying and comforting influence of the Holy Spirit.

> "*The comfort flows plentifully and constantly as a river, strong as a stream to bear down the opposition of doubts and fears. There is a fullness in Christ, of grace for grace. The Spirit dwelling and working in believers is as a fountain of living, running water, out of which plentiful streams flow, cooling and cleansing as water. The miraculous gifts of the Holy Spirit we do not expect, but for his more common and more valuable influences we may apply. These streams have flowed from our glorified Redeemer, down to this age, and to the remote corners of the earth."* [34] (Matthew Henry)

The blessing of a restored relationship with Christ comes with the dwelling of the Holy Spirit. It was described and related to living water because of the revival effect and new hope that's anchored in grace.

---

[34] John 7:38. Matthew Henry Concise Commentary. www.biblehub.com

It was expressed as "rivers of living water" because of our overflowing experience of grace. Such living flow is so overflowing that it affects others. Here, we somewhat understood why there are instances in which God allowed us to experience challenges and trials. It is not for our destruction but for us to realize our shortcomings and weakness, and from such, we'd learn and be encouraged to depend more on Christ and the power of the Holy Spirit. At the same time, we're encouraged to move forward despite our weaknesses because the grace of God empowers us, and the Holy Spirit helps us to be no longer enslaved by sin.

Moving forward to the third verse, John 8:38, this verse contributes to the truth of Jesus' unity with God.

> *"I speak the things which I have seen with My Father; therefore you also do the things which you heard from your father." (John 8:38, NASB1995)*

Jesus Christ opposed the arrogance and vain confidence of the people (Abraham's descendants). Christ shows that their connection with Abraham will not be profitable, particularly those who question His existence as God's sent Messiah. In our lives today, we tend to disregard the truth and Jesus' modeling, thinking that it's more viable to rely on someone who currently lived and demonstrated experiences.

I (Annie) remember when I asked Rey's permission to join this small business network, and I had to pay $750/month just to be part of it. The fees covered exclusive discussions, sharing ideas with the top Cs of other local small businesses (CEO, COO, and CFO), and monthly learnings from an expert. The idea was good, but the fees were an additional challenge for someone struggling to keep the business floating like us. This could be a good investment if the company has extra funds to dispose of. As Rey continued asking for the planned topics that would be shared, he pointed out those topics that I already learned when I took my MBA. There could be differences when knowledge is shared with experiences. Yet, at that particular moment, we knew we needed accountability that would drive us to a more profound encouragement and courage for bold actions toward significant changes. Nowadays, there are some ways to achieve business accountability and free from programs of non-profit organizations, but we have to seek that "profound encouragement." Little did we know that we would have such from Jesus Christ. Not until we realize that God primarily owns the business and we're just stewards of this blessing will we continue to search for "profound encouragement."

I (Rey) declined the job, and we planned to work together to keep up the business. The job will affect the weekend that Annie and I decided to commit ourselves for our intentionality in this journey. We were already loaded from business operations to children's school and other weekday activities back then. The weekend is our only solid shot to engage them and be intentional in this new life journey as a family. We knew we'd have some adjustments, mainly as we dealt with the complexity of our family - that's our top priority, and that's our primary ministry. I knew we had many revisions as I felt the business was too damaged. Yet, in deciding to decline the job and give much attention to the company, I was firmly convinced upon seeking God's guidance through His words. Such conviction will only be validated when God reveals things in due time. For now, our role is to continue to seek Christ and experience that all blessings are from God (1 Corinthians 9:8-10). If our ways follow God's, we'll hold on to the truth that only through Him will our ways be established (Proverbs 3:5- 6).

After carefully discussing our next steps, I (Annie) devoted some time to fully understanding the business's current condition from the perspectives of finance, sales, marketing, and operations. I prepared thorough information about the company, not in the format that I prefer but with the intention of Rey's understanding. After all the information was laid out, we created some plans, and our goal is to continue to seek God's affirmation and guidance in every step we take. We've considered closing the business and getting him a job that could offer a better schedule. Despite the limited resources, we also planned the necessary steps to rehabilitate the company immediately. It was a struggle, but the battle was like facing our fears and doubts. We disciplined ourselves to sit down and discuss things even when there were moments when our buttons were pressed because of the stress. I'll pray to overcome fear upon checking work emails, for every new design to be released, for every moment I have to update our financial report, for every marketing strategy decision we make, and for the amount of funds to be released. Our family established a habit of nightly praying and regularly discussing God's words because we know that every step of the way is motivated by the desire to obey Him.

As we shared in Chapter 2, God may have saved our hearts and restored our relationship with Him through Jesus Christ. Little do we know that our restored faith in God covers every facet of our marriage. At this defining moment, our collected encounter in God's words lets us experience what it's like to have a marriage united under the banner of Jesus Christ. Since we both long for His guidance and commit ourselves to seek His ways continually, purpose, and will, we're already blessed to experience His presence alone in our marriage.

Despite our efforts, we're not observing any significant progression in the business. Although God's words were consistent in our devotions—be still, take courage, and depend on Him—there were many moments when He reminded us of His promises. Yet, our stubbornness has led us to consider seeking legal advice on closing the business since it's not making significant progress. We anticipated our future steps and took the paperwork we needed to complete. For some reason, on that particular week, we received a substantial volume of orders that delayed our time completing the paperwork. As we're in the process of fulfilling the order, the Governor of Nevada announced a State of Emergency due to COVID-19.

(Annie's Journal Entry dated March 20, 2020)

"It's been four days of "stay-home-care," because of the virus. There is non-stop overwhelming news throughout the day, even in the previous days. Despite this situation, God is showing us His protection and faithfulness. All the pressure from our financial side has been put on hold, and tax filing has been extended from April 15th to July 15th, giving me much time to work on the paperwork. Surprisingly, we're still receiving some orders."

We all know how things have changed during those lockdowns. We tried to seek help, particularly on the business side, but we didn't receive enough to give us considerable space to rehabilitate. The amount we received was enough to keep us moving on a smaller scale. Many thought this lockdown would not last that long, but it took some significant time. Considering the non-essential qualifications of our products, we may have gone deeper if we had pushed for higher funding during that time. We're just thankful that our response was to be grateful to God and manage diligently what we only have. There were moments when income was not enough to cover everything. Our attempt to communicate and submit payments on the amount we can afford didn't go through to some entities. We fully understood them as those times were very critical.

We just moved forward on the system that we know was pleasing to God. We honored Him in every blessing we received. There are moments when we're bothered, but if we can't do anything about it, we sincerely come to God for comfort and courage to move forward. Even on a smaller business scale during that pandemic, we're able to close three small personal loans and two business cash advances. God indeed provided when we needed to catch up on our mortgage. The pandemic also allowed us to be more engaged with the children. We embraced homeschooling, a new learning moment for us as parents.

Although there was an evident struggle to juggle responsibilities, during that season, we initially experienced unity in our family and worked accordingly on our necessary tasks.

Looking back on our situation a few months before the lockdown, we see that the pandemic would have thwarted our plans. The job that I (Rey) could have accepted would have been short-lived because the company laid off its most recent hires and prioritized those who had been with them for specific significant years. The time we devoted to fully understanding the business and our situation in terms of financial matters helped and equipped us during the lockdown period. Many offers were tempting during the early lockdown period because many anticipated it would be short, but God's conviction and discernment protected us. Even after the lockdown and the world's transition to "affected normal," the economy was still in a critical adjustment period that was challenging to many small business owners like us. We thanked God for His protection, shielding us from further consequences.

Turning pandemic as opportunity to embrace homeschooling

God will allow circumstances in our lives so we can have a genuine experience of the reality of His words and His presence. As we observed His unified message, we experienced how it is to be united with God as the center of our marriage. This redefining moment didn't just solidify our dependence on His words. It changed how we view His messages and anchor them in our relationship.

CHAPTER 7
IT'S ALL ABOUT THE HEART

Our collective encounters with God have helped us stay focused on pursuing Christ in our lives and marriage. We've witnessed how God is gradually transforming us and our situation, so even when we encounter bumps, we know that we need to hold on to God tighter and firmer. We're experiencing God's hands as He helps us to strengthen our partnership in this journey. Even in moments that we haven't seen a wholly answered prayer in some of our concerns, we're getting opportunities and chances to overcome our fears and doubts. He's helping us to better our communication and be intentional in our regular spiritual discussions. The continuing discussion of such a journey happens in our household - over dinner, nightly praying time, homeschooling, and weekly "Sabbath Day." We didn't have such intentional experiences when we were growing up, so every opportunity given to us is all by God's grace. It's not always that things are working out fine. Even today, we're still in the process of learning—our regular recount of the manifestations of God's grace, mercy, and love in our lives. We know and understand that Christianity is not a storm-free life. It is God's promised new life that's stormproof and able to experience the reality of His existence and the powerful message of Jesus' sacrifice on the cross. The reality of sacrifices in following Christ (Matthew 16:24-26, Luke 9:57-62) becomes also Satan's playground, so we will be discouraged, delayed, or worse, totally lose our heart in our connection with God.

119

In Chapter 5, we shared our ordeal of learning the brokenness of this world, the weakness of our flesh, and the existence of evil. This understanding should not lead us to passivity but must serve as a powerful reminder to stay firmly anchored in Christ as we continue our journey. This includes strengthening our connection to the power of the Holy Spirit. In John 16:33, Jesus Christ highlighted the importance of our connection with Him as we journey this life, and it is only through Him that we can find true peace, even amid tribulation.

> *"These things I have spoken to you, so that in Me you may have peace. In the world you have tribulation, but take courage; I have overcome the world."* (John 16:33, NASB1995)

This last verse of John 16 concludes Christ's teaching to His disciples. Interestingly, Jesus Christ remarks, *"In the world you have tribulation."* The emphasis on the reality of "tribulation" in the world should encourage His disciples (and us, Christ-followers, today) to stay anchored in Him. We can understand further the great importance of this verse by reflecting on the previous verses in this chapter - His warning (John 16:1-4), the promise of the Holy Spirit (John 16:5-15), the foretold of His death and resurrection (John 16:16-22) and the promise of prayers (John 16:23-28).

The *"Tribulation"* in verse 33 is from the Greek word [35]thlibó, which means afflicted, distressing, or suffering affliction.

---

[35] Strong's Concordance, www.biblehub.com

We usually think that the antidote for affliction is to get out of it, yet in this verse, Jesus noted that we should take courage, and in some Bible translations, it is *"take heart."* If we check the original Greek translation of this courage, [36]tharsos, it is similar to the usage for confidence. We can safely conclude that Jesus wants us to have courage and confidence in our hearts when facing the tribulations in this world.

Sadly, the reality of *"tribulation"* has become confusing and challenging for many of us to connect with God's goodness and omnipotence. The most common question is, if God is good and all-powerful, why is there tribulation that brings pain to us? Why is there still conflict in our family? We wish we could confidently say we've grasped the understanding required in this matter immediately, but it took some time, and we must constantly remind ourselves. It's a continuous process of learning. Translating our personal experiences and attempting to communicate with others doesn't always go well. It requires in-depth appropriation and proper timing paralleled with compassion wrapped in the power of the Holy Spirit so that the message will be communicated lovingly and accepted in reflection of God's grace. The sensitivity of pain that resulted from tribulation and the required firmness in God's characters are evident in our responses toward these contrasting yet very related truths. Why is that so?

In our desire to understand pain and suffering, we refer to C.S. Lewis' book, *"The Problem of Pain."*[37]

---

[36] Strong's Concordance, www.biblehub.com

[37] Lewis, C. S. 1. (2001). *The Problem of Pain.* First HarperCollins paperback edition. New York, NY, HarperOne.

The book seeks to understand how a loving, good, and powerful God can coexist with the pain and suffering in the world and our lives. Lewis didn't go straight in discussing human pain. We can see Lewis' attempt to establish in readers the foundational truths of God's divine omnipotence and goodness, as well as the apparent reality of human wickedness and the fall of man. Sadly, there's an evident disconnection to these truths because of the continuous wrong perception of Christianity. We thought our troubled lives would turn upside down once we qualified ourselves as "Christians." God indeed promised us a good life (Jeremiah 29:11). Still, our ignorance and intent avoidance of the problem of pain disregard the reality of the Christian journey and the truth behind man's natural continuous battle of sin. So we thought Christianity would save us from pain when, in fact, we'll experience more so we can understand it and better equip ourselves to guard our hearts.

> *"(Christianity) It is not a system into which we have to fit the awkward fact of pain: it is itself one of the awkward facts which have to be fitted into any system we make. In a sense, it creates, rather than solves, the problem of pain, for pain would be no problem unless, side by side with our daily experience of this painful of this world, we had received what we think a good assurance that ultimate reality is righteous and loving."* [38](C.S. Lewis, "The Problem of Pain")

The intuitive relationship between God's existence (with emphasis on His attributes - divine omnipotence and divine goodness) and pain must be correctly understood, that is, if

---

[38] Lewis, C. S. 1. (2001). *The Problem of Pain*. First HarperCollins paperback edition. New York, NY, HarperOne.

we're honestly confronting the complex issues that lie within. Faith risks deteriorating if we're not letting ourselves in such understanding. We're moving forward with moral blindness and a heart not properly guarded in pain. We're falling into the dangerous wagon of wrong perspective about Christianity. Dr. Peter Tan-chi of Christ Commission Fellowship constantly notes;

> *"Christianity is not about perfection, rather living an authentic life with Jesus Christ."* [39](Dr. Peter Tan-Chi)

Christianity is not about achieving a "perfect" state of life but an authentic journey with Christ Jesus. Our relationship with Jesus encourages and convicts us of our shortcomings and weaknesses, giving us more courage to lean more on God's grace and the power of the Holy Spirit. We'll be guided and guarded when facing the reality of our shortcomings. Sadly, our ignorance or wrong perspective puts us in many unguarded, vulnerable instances that we've become Satan's object, and he continually uses pain so he can further create more until the division is imminent. The dangerous thing is that we often think of this thing in a bigger context, where, in reality, Satan is actively doing it to the smallest unit - the family, and ensuring the destruction of its foundation - the husband and wife.

Before we completely dive into the pain problem, let's revisit the Biblical definition of our being (human—God's creature) that's highly impacted by this pain—our hearts. It's not a common topic of discussion how the Bible truly defined the status of our hearts.

---

[39] Tan-chi, P. Christ Commission Fellowship. https://www.ccf.org.ph

Maybe because we're not honest enough to admit the real condition of the very core part of ourselves. Thinking that we have a certain capacity to hide and move forward with this life, projecting that we're adapting very well. The truth is that the Bible describes the human heart as (1) evil (Genesis 6:5, Genesis 8:21) and (2) deceitful and wicked (Jeremiah 17:9).

> *"Then the Lord saw that the wickedness of man was great on the earth, and that every intent of the thoughts of **his heart was only evil continually.**"* (Genesis 6:5, NASB1995)

> *"The Lord smelled the soothing aroma; and the Lord said to Himself, 'I will never again curse the ground on account of man, for the intent of **man's heart is evil** from his youth; and I will never again destroy every living thing, as I have done."* (Genesis 8:21, NASB1995)

God sees all human wickedness, which cannot be concealed from Him. He observed that the fountain of sin is in hearts. Even in a brief moment when there is an attempt to declare goodness, He sees any hidden wickedness in the imagination of thoughts and emotions built within the heart. It is a sad sight for God and very offensive in His holiness. The second Biblical description of man's heart is that it is deceitful, crooked, polluted, or simply cannot be trusted.

> *"**The heart is more deceitful** than all else and is desperately sick; who can understand it?"* (Jeremiah 17:9. NASB1995)

We're not strangers on this matter. We've sinned, and there is a continuous battle of sin. Even in the effort of declaring that we trust God, there's a part in our hearts that we're expecting blessings - a belief of a promise that's naturally installed in our hearts. On the other hand, the declaration of trust is not evident in our succeeding actions. Just like in moments when we've claimed that we're seeking God and His guidance, amid challenges, we'll move forward anxious and settle on the ways that we thought would be quicker or more comfortable on our side. We think we trust God when our hopes and fears rise and fall in second that circumstances wiggle our sincere declaration of trust. As Matthew Henry commented,

> *"We think that we trust in God when we do not, as appears by this, that our hopes and fears rise or fall, as second causes smiles of frown... There is wickedness in our hearts which we are not aware of and do not suspect to be there; nay, it is a common mistake among the children of men to think themselves, their hearts at least, a great deal better than they are... God knows more evil of us than we do of ourselves, which is a good reason why we should not flatter ourselves but always stand in awe of the judgment of God."*
> [40](Matthew Henry)

That's the reality of our heart's condition, and we often find ways not to put the reality in light because of shame or possibly fear, so we'll cover it up as much as we can. The saddest truth is sometimes we're not fully aware of how wounded our hearts are from the pain collected over years of unprocessed experiences of afflictions and sufferings.

---

[40] Henry, M. (n.d.). Matthew Henry Commentary. *Blue Letter Bible.* https://www.blueletterbible.org/

The Evangelist - J. John from London noted;

> *"The heart of the human problem is the problem of the human heart."* [41](J.John)

Our hearts are wounded and may still face more wounds in the future because of the reality of the world's brokenness, the weakness of our flesh, and evil's existence. Most of the time, we're not fully aware of how wounded it is because we've become callous about the behavior and perspective that developed through these wounds. Also, many are unaware that our wounds could be deeper than our convictions. We're not innocent on these. While working on this book, that's when we only had a good opportunity to review ourselves and relate to the truth about our heart's condition and pain problem. Our fascination with the collected wisdom from gifted experts is truly a blessing. Relating that wisdom and knowledge to our experiences has provided a good level of understanding and an accountability opportunity for improved responses, particularly towards pain and suffering.

In C.S. Lewis' book, *"The Problem of Pain,"* he mentioned the two senses of pain: [42](1) a particular kind of sensation, probably conveyed by specialized nerve fibers, and recognizable by the patient as the kind of sensation whether dislikes or not, and (2) any experience (physical or mental) that's synonymous with suffering, anguish, tribulation,

---

[41] J. John. (2024, August 15). Reasons to believe in Jesus [Video]. YouTube; Focus on the Family. https://www.youtube.com

[42]. Lewis, C. S. 1. (2001). The problem of pain. First HarperCollins paperback edition. New York, NY, HarperOne.

adversity or trouble. Lewis's discussion in this book is directed more toward the pain experienced from tribulation, adversity, etc., and he shared the three suffering operations.

1. Three Operations of Suffering | Pain is unmasked, unmistakable evil

Many think that when we're in pain, something is wrong, and it is purely negative, denying any potential positive aspects or necessary functions of pain. For believers, the grace of God and the power of the Holy Spirit help them view these sufferings as God's assignment or season of learning.

"God whispers to us in our pleasures, speaks in our conscience but shouts in our pain: it is His megaphone to rouse a deaf world." [43](C.S. Lewis, "The Problem of Pain")

On the other hand, "judgment" is quick to manifest in minds and then translate to words upon witnessing or receiving news of suffering, whether sudden or not. Come to think of it, man's generational approach led us to a poor perception of pain as unmistakable evil. In the book, Lewis shared his childhood experience with his brother about the jerked elbow that caused him to make an irrelevant line across the middle of his drawing work. His brother was allowed to draw a similar line to Lewis' work to reach an amicable settlement. This reminded us of similar childhood experiences and our parenting today. When one takes offensive words or actions toward the other, we're quick to apply punishment so the house will return to quietness or calmness.

---

[43] Lewis, C. S. 1. (2001). *The Problem of Pain*. First HarperCollins paperback edition. New York, NY, HarperOne.

A better approach could be a teaching moment for children to deal with pain by discussing the incident and reaching an understanding that continues even when applying the punishment. The punishment required serves as training because of the wrong actions (Proverbs 22:6). The objective is not to repeat the same mistake or at least remember the consequences so it will drive to a better decision. Of course, the discussion will be challenging at children's certain age level. Still, the intentionality of paying some attention first to the hurt child to soothe the hurt, then working with the child who took the offense afterward, could be possible. Then, be there and help them return to enjoy playing games again. In this manner, we're allowing the children to witness and practice taking time (or pause) to deal with pain and not letting it affect their relationship and back to the happiness of reconciliation. As they grow and can handle the conversation, we can include the importance of having a relationship with Jesus Christ and leaning to the influence of the Holy Spirit when the reality of behavior and personality differences tend to push the buttons of disagreements and conflicts. We wish we'd known this before. Things could have been different, but thank God as He graciously opens opportunities today. Opportunities to navigate sufferings, not in the context of evil's action but learning about God's action towards our brokenness. If we let our minds settle on this perspective, there's a higher chance that our responses to suffering that causes pain to someone will lean more on compassion rather than evil's work of judgment. Even amid required discussion to achieve understanding, grace is noticeable because we know that everyone has shortcomings and fellow recipient of God's grace. We'd learn to be compassionate (Romans 12:15) and have the opportunity to carry each other's burden in the existence of pain while facing God's divine appointed season for the sanctification process (Galatians 6:2-5). This is not an easy response for many of us because by nature we tend to protect ourselves from any sudden pain that we'll encounter. Either we'll keep ourselves in a "safe position" or we'll fight back. The painful life circumstances that I (Rey) had, combined with the military training that I lived for 20 years are sitting in my inner self are indeed a combo of a big struggle on this matter. Truly, everything boils down to our relationship with Jesus Christ, fear in God, and the Holy Spirit's dominant influence. It is indeed a difficult process of transformation but we have a living hope, Jesus Christ, who didn't just promise deliverance but continuous guidance.

2. Three Operations of Suffering | Pain leads us to seek happiness in God

"Everyone has noticed how hard it is to turn our thoughts to God when everything is going well with us. We 'have all we want' is a terrible saying when "all" does not include God. We find God an interruption." [44](C.S. Lewis, "The Problem of Pain")

When God or anything related to Him is nowhere in our definition of happiness or object of happiness, we'll struggle to learn that we can only find genuine happiness through and in Him alone. Seeking Him in the season of suffering will be challenging, and it will require His divine orchestration so our hearts will sincerely and genuinely do so.

---

[44] Lewis, C. S. 1. (2001). *The Problem of Pain*. First HarperCollins paperback edition. New York, NY, HarperOne.

Despite a good collection of recorded stories in the Bible, we're letting ignorance or unwillingness miss the opportunities to learn to navigate pain and seek God for happiness. Instead, we let ourselves be drawn to the world's offering of temporal happiness. Whether it's an object (money, house, cars, etc.) or earthly relationships (like a spouse, children, relatives, friends, etc.), we've let ourselves attached to something visible, that can reciprocate our expectations or something in "acceptable-level" of endurance that we can withstand. It became the center of our hearts, and we relied on happiness. The next thing you know, it turned into a controlling factor that replaces God's position in our hearts.

When I (Annie) met Rey, the complications of our situation didn't hinder me from being hopeful for him, our relationship, and our intended future together. I was elated when I witnessed things slowly falling into place, and we're adapting to our new life here in the US. My happiness towards him and our relationship was established because of our equally shared commitment to building the family we both desired. Even when disagreement will pass by, we're able to manage to get through with it and continue to move forward. Yet, when our family started to experience deeper disagreements and overwhelming complications (as shared in Chapter 1), my happiness was nowhere to be found. God intercepted and turned things around in how we view ourselves as husband and wife. My joy was restored, but I didn't expect to be tested in this area. I understood the conflicts would continue to exist or attempt to affect our relationship significantly. Still, I didn't expect God would allow a particular incident that led me to question my faith and trust in Him. As well as have a more profound heart check in the avenue of earthly relationships and my restored relationship with Him. It was a harrowing season that even our regular discussion as husband and wife was tested. I experienced anger and fear. I sounded prideful and selfish. The spiritual battle was so intense that I mostly lay in bed in a dark room and cried to God. I told myself, *"So this could be how Job felt."*

The grieving continued but was interrupted as more conflicts and trials decided to fall in the same season. My (Annie's) attempt to get attention for help and understanding failed, and instead, I received more condemnation and judgment. Maybe it's not, but Satan was so vital to convey those attempts to lose traces of grace. The overwhelming turn of events was not gracious enough to give me space to breathe or to grieve completely. It didn't give me many options but to isolate myself and surrender those pains to God. Not for the sake of unwillingness to honestly admit the pain and difficulty of challenges, but hoping for disconnection will not create further misunderstandings. So, I finally told God that if I (and our family) had to go through this, I begged for His mercy and grace.

I've (Annie) never experienced nor expected such darkness in the same season we decided to commit ourselves to God, so the pain harshly stubbed a deep wound. Those days with uncontrolled tears, Rey shared gestures of loving comfort, yet surprisingly, it wasn't as impactful as it used to be. Maybe because both of our hearts were heavily burdened, or my sinful heart still holds blame towards him. I asked God for comfort in His words, and when I requested His presence to reassure me that we're not alone in this battle, He was so gracious to do so. In an unexpected moment when I couldn't hold back the tears (again), God blessed me with a sister-in-Christ who quietly held my hands. I didn't hear any words, and she just remained on my side, crying with me. At that moment, I knew it was God's orchestration that I would surprisingly experience the reassurance that we're not alone in this battle, even when such a battle crushed my spirit for a moment.

"The Lord is near to the brokenhearted and saves those who are crushed in spirit." (Psalms 34:18, NASB1995)

At that moment, when I (Annie) was deeply struggling, my Bible reading habit fell on the chapters of Psalm. I thank God that even through His words, He orchestrated the timing. David's vulnerable season recorded in those Psalms has become my comforting words and grounded me to seek and trust God. We all know how David had his own painful experience in relationships (2 Samuel 15), and he boldly expressed his pain through Psalms (Psalm 55:12-15). My stretched thread of trusting God was strengthened through words in Psalms. I concluded my journey in reading this book with a note that I wrote in my Bible;

"If our lives don't reflect the words we're singing, we're not authentically worshiping God."

We, believers, love to declare our devotion and trust to God through singing. But when we're amid adversity, are these lyrics deeply rooted in our hearts that we can still find happiness with Him despite suffering in pain? Can we still worship God and give Him glory even amid a bleeding and deeply wounded heart?

3. Three Operations of Suffering | Pain teaches us self-sacrifice and that we're finally acting for God's sake

"If the thing we like doing is in fact, the thing God wants us to do, yet that is not our reason for doing it, it remains a mere happy coincidence. We cannot, therefore, know that we are acting at all, or primarily, for God's sake, unless the material of the action is contrary to our inclinations or (in other words) painful, and what we cannot know that we are choosing, we cannot choose." [45] (C.S. Lewis, "The Problem of Pain")

In this part of his book, Lewis makes a very compelling comment. This comment recognizes and describes the possible moral blindness in living a life that serves God. He also pointed out the reality of sacrifices in obeying God to offer a life that genuinely serves Him. Lewis then noted that we can only be sure we're acting for God's sake when our actions come against our natural desire or can be defined as complex. This is quite a good reminder of when Jesus Christ declared that He arrived to do the will of God, the Father (John 6:37-39). Even on such obedience, He knew it would cost His earthly body to die on the cross (Mark 9:30-32). Speaking to His disciples then (which applies to us all today as well), if we decide to follow Him, we should be willing to deny ourselves, take up the cross, and follow Him (Matthew 16:24-26). This clearly explains that recognizing our own life with God's authority is crucial in terms of free will and intentionality.

---

[45] Lewis, C. S. 1. (2001). *The Problem of Pain*. First HarperCollins paperback edition. New York, NY, HarperOne.

Lewis suggested that true choice requires conscious awareness of what we're choosing and why. If we fail to distinguish between acting for God and acting for our own pleasure, we're not really choosing to serve God.

Jesus Christ is the ultimate example of obeying God's will, yet the Bible records many others who've decided to obey God and displayed profound sacrifices. Apostle Paul mentioned a good rundown of faithful God's servants when talking to the Hebrews (Hebrews 11). Then, Apostle Paul encouraged them to lay aside every burden and entanglement of sin and patiently endure the race of this life with fixed eyes on Jesus Christ.

> *"Therefore, since we have so great a cloud of witnesses surrounding us, let us also lay aside every encumbrance and the sin which so easily entangles us, and let us run with endurance the race that is set before us, fixing our eyes on Jesus, the author and perfecter of faith, who for the joy set before Him endured the cross, despising the shame, and has sat down at the right hand of the throne of God."* (Hebrews 12:1-2, NASB1995)

When we learn of the reality of sacrifices in Christianity, we would surely think this is impossible. It is indeed impossible! It's not a natural inclination for us (humans) to sacrifice ourselves; by nature, we're selfish and prideful. There's an evident wrestle in sin. Even Apostle Paul complained;

> *"For what I am doing, I do not understand; for I am not practicing what I would like to do, but I am doing the very thing I hate."* (Romans 7:15, NASB1995)

We can feel the Apostle Paul's words here. However, we should be cautious about taking this message into giving further excuses to take Christianity into lighter consideration and just move on "soft-pedaling" the reality of sin. Instead, let's take these words as a humbling message reflecting the reality of our flesh, a sinful one. As we get closer to God and know His attributes, we see more of our sins. That's why we'd see the great importance of the sanctification process—a process of conforming to Christlikeness where our nature is leaning in the strength of the Holy Spirit. Matthew Henry's commentary on these words of Apostle Paul covers the reality of our flesh nature and the participation of sin, which encourages us to surrender to God fully;

> *"And many believers have adopted the apostle's language, showing that it is suitable to their deep feelings of abhorrence of sin, and self-abasement. The apostle enlarges on the conflict he daily maintained with the remainder of his original depravity. He was frequently led into tempers, words, or actions, which he did not approve of or allow in his renewed judgment and affections. By distinguishing his real self, his spiritual part, from the self, or flesh, in which sin dwelt, and by observing that the evil actions were done, not by him, but by sin dwelling in him, the apostle did not mean that men are not accountable for their sins, but he teaches the evil of their sins, by showing that they are all done against reason and conscience. Sin dwelling in a man does not prove its ruling, or having dominion over him. If a man dwells in a city or a country, still he may not rule there."* [46](Matthew Henry)

---

[46] Henry, M. (n.d.). Matthew Henry Commentary. *Bible Hub.* https://www.biblehub.com

It breaks my (Rey's) heart to witness Annie grieving and see the reflection of pain in the eyes of our children. It was indeed a very dark season for us. If my "old self" existed in this situation, I would ignore it and leave. Yet, my fear of God has changed my heart's desire when facing difficult situations. I realized how wrong I was in doing nothing when finding myself in conflicts, just like those times of my previous marriages' conflicts, and quickly relied on divorce for a quick escape. Realizing such was indeed a significant factor in my third marriage, and taking action for a change wasn't easy apart from God. As I got to know God, my view and approach to conflict have somewhat evolved, and this is one of the things Annie and I agreed to change in our household. We have to discuss it and deal with it right away. The encouragement is to pause, pray, and ask the Holy Spirit for the courage to speak the truth and admit participation in any conflict. The timely approach in handling misunderstandings, disagreements, and disputes is a great help not to be Satan's object for any intent division. It's not an easy practice and often leads to a very uncomfortable discussion. In the end, we chose to rely on God and pray. There were moments when I gave all the credit to the Holy Spirit, yet there were also instances when my anger and temper were evident. So it's an every day begging to God for forgiveness and guidance.

Our desire to have a different life that serves God and willingness to take such pain for God's sake is mainly viewed in a church context when, in reality, it should start in our household. As you've seen in the previous chapter, we shared how we made decisions and what drove us to anchor our lives to God intentionally. However, Annie and I (Rey) are first on both sides of the families that decided to be intentional in our Christian walk and embrace discipleship. Our journey to Christianity indeed put us in painful realities of our sinfulness and deciding to take actions that are against our natural heart's desire. It is truly a conflict of "two natures" - God's righteousness and man's sinful nature. Only by God's grace were our eyes enlightened on the wrongdoings and the conviction in our hearts that we submit to God's authority and have the courage to face our shortcomings. Indeed, the roles and responsibilities that God entrusted to us (fellow married men) of being leaders (and spiritual leaders) to our wives (and children) bring us to a journey of continuous battle in sin - tempted by a natural desire to put matters in our own hands and failure to seek God's will and ways. Indeed, we will find ourselves on the edge of sacrificing our own will, just like this recent dark season that we had to go through. The heavy burden in my heart was a mixture of grief and anger. My attempt to reach an understanding has failed, leaving me no option but to ask God for answers. Annie tried to help. I can see her sincerity in helping me out, but her attempts to share Bible verses, related podcast episodes, or preaching episodes on YouTube have turned out to be "pushy." I told her I have so many questions in my heart that I'm asking God for clarity through His words. As much as I want a discussion to reach an understanding and amicable resolution, it is tricky and complicated if the willingness is inconsistent with everyone. It was sad to let ourselves be cornered in any avenue of conflict, but maybe this time, I needed to pause and seek God more.

When I (Annie) saw that my attempts for help were not working, I ended up on my knees, begging God for help. I boldly prayed to God on how painful it is to be distant with my husband. We've been on that road, and God delivered us already, yet suddenly, there's strong blurriness in our once clear, united hearts. I've seen many moments when Rey broke down in God's conviction and powerful messages through His words, but why is it so challenging to see such an encounter or not even get closer to that in this very critical season? Then, God strongly spoke to me through His words. I'm finally reminded and convicted that my actions in such a moment don't translate to understanding. I failed to provide an understanding of his actions and plan as our spiritual leader of the family. I was unable to provide understanding as his partner in our business. I failed to give an understanding of his desire to obey God's call to serve. I was unable to share understanding in this critical moment as a fellow Christ-follower. Upon receiving such a conviction, I immediately asked Rey for forgiveness. I intentionally devoted the succeeding days to two ways of listening - (1) emotions and (2) facts, that aim for understanding. Jesus Christ showed how listening is critical for understanding when He was sharing parables. In Matthew 13:13-15, He showed that we can be callous in listening and fall to misunderstanding. So for us to reach such an understanding we need to sincerely listen with our ears and understand with our hearts. Also, Solomon a very good wisdom in terms of knowledge and understanding. Our sincere actions to fill ourselves with knowledge may offer practical applications that could build, but it's only through understanding it is established (Proverbs 24:3).

When God's reminder of "understanding" captured our attention, it paved the way for us to look deeper into our hearts. We don't usually give ourselves time to evaluate our hearts. We've become too busy attending to each role this life offered us. But if we sincerely have a "heart check," we'll recognize how significantly the heart affects our minds and actions. Even the capability to act well amid pressured situations is still related to a heart condition. This just shows us a good glimpse of why God wants our hearts. This is not in a sense that refers to devotion to "religious acts," but instead, God wants a heart that translates actions, perspectives, and emotions into a message of His grace, which Jesus stated in John 7:38.

Our journey of "heart-check" helped us understand our personalities and behavior, which are very significant to our hearts' emotions. When we accepted Jesus Christ as our personal Lord and Savior, we took that gift of Salvation that includes His forgiveness and healing process of our past brokenness. Little did we know that declaration considerably unveils how broken our hearts are, and we have learned how this heart responds to future pains that are essential in our journey. Well, it just makes a sensible thought that for us to experience God's healing, He will reveal the areas we need healing. Apparently, there are certain broken factors that we're fully aware of. Maybe because of pride or we got used to avoiding such for a long time that we've become callous about it.

We're both strong-willed people, evident in our personalities and behaviors. Differences arise because of our opposite personalities. One (Rey) is an introvert who gives himself time to think and process things by being quiet. Once his (Rey's) thoughts are collected, he'll open his mouth. The other (Annie) is an extrovert who talks while processing her thoughts. If we give ourselves some time to analyze the flow from heart to mind to mouth. We'll notice how being "strong-willed" or "submissive" affects our behavior related to our personalities (extrovert or introvert). So the main thing is, what is the focus object of our being strong-willed or submissive? What motivates or triggers us to be strong-willed or submissive? Is such an "object" related or anchored to God? We must understand what happens in our hearts when we used to live a life separated from God and what kind of behavior builds up during such a season. So, we'll have a good sense of self-awareness and be intentional in seeking God's guidance for the complete healing of our wounded hearts. As the Bible says, we must guard our hearts (Proverbs 4:23). How can we guard something we're unaware of?

Both clinical psychologists and known Christian counselors, (late) Dr. David Stoop and his wife, Dr. Jan Stoop, have written a very interesting book, [47]*"The Emotionally Healthy Marriage."* The book aims to provide understanding and practical guidance for couples to grow closer by understanding each other. They mentioned that emotions are closest to our innermost being and bring technicolor to our lives. Researchers and experts generally agree that we're experiencing six primary emotions: anger, sadness, joy, surprise, shame (sometimes called disgust), and fear. The Stoops mentioned that love doesn't appear on the list. In most literature related to EQ and business, love is never discussed because of its complexity, and it covers a lot of territory.[48]

---

[47] J Stoop, D., & Stoop, J. (2020). *The Emotionally Healthy Marriage: Growing Closer by Understanding One Another*. Revell of Baker Publishing Group.

[48] J Stoop, D., & Stoop, J. (2020). *The Emotionally Healthy Marriage: Growing Closer by Understanding One Another*. Revell of Baker Publishing Group.

This doesn't mean that the feeling of love is viewed poorly, but those six primary emotions are the immediate expression when someone encounters vulnerability and triggers emotion. The book presented a comprehensive analysis of emotions and illustrated a good collection of practical applications that will surely be helpful for married couples. These practical applications follow the acronym guide they've created - [49]S.M.A.R.T. *(Self-awareness of your emotions; Managing your emotions; Accountability to yourself, your spouse, and others; Reading the other person's emotions; Together in the land of emotions).* The table below defines this acronym, and we added some Biblical principles that we find will be helpful for us in relating this practical concept to our life today.

Self-awareness of your emotions	*Apostle Paul encouraged us in Romans 12:3 to have a right and modest view of ourselves and be aware of whether we're setting ourselves in high regard or moderating our attitudes. Emotion has become a vital medium for how we want to regard ourselves.*
Managing your emotions	*The Bible has many verses that tell us how to manage our emotions, like being slow to anger (James 1:19-20, Ephesians 4:26-27) or being full of joy (Philippians 4:4-8). The Bible recognizes our emotions; they exist, and we'll experience them, but the main command is that we should be filled with the Holy Spirit in dealing with these emotions (Romans 6; Ephesians 5:15-18; 1 Peter 5:6-11).*

---

[49]J Stoop, D., & Stoop, J. (2020). *The Emotionally Healthy Marriage: Growing Closer by Understanding One Another*. Revell of Baker Publishing Group.

Accountability to yourself, your spouse, and others	We're all accountable to God (Hebrews 4:13; Romans 14:12), and the Bible is also evident in the encouragement for mutual accountability (Colossians 3:16; James 5:16)
Reading the other person's emotions	Reading for the objective of understanding and not with something else so we can share an empathy that's pleasing to God (Romans 12:15).
Together in the land of emotions	One of the great blessings in marriage anchored in God is having a partner navigating emotions. The Bible has many verses encouraging us to live in harmony with one another (like in Romans 12:16). Solomon shared in Ecclesiastes 4:9-12 of having a partner and emphasized how great sorrow can turn into a blessing between two individuals in verse 10.

The book has many beautiful insights, but the one that immediately captured our attention is the discussion of BEP (Basic Emotional Posture), according to Drs. Stoops, we typically choose to go to one of the basic four emotions (anger, fear, sadness, and shame) when we're under stress or when someone has pushed our buttons. Identifying and understanding our fallback emotion will involve some historical remembering [50]. Upon learning this BEP, we took our heart check discussion to the roots of our automatic responses. This gave us a clear view of our unconscious behavior, established over time from ignored or unprocessed painful experiences. We reviewed our reactions toward each other and how our emotions have become Satan's playground, so we'll lose track of our common goal and delay God's intent for us and our

---

[50] Stoop, D., & Stoop, J. (2020). *The Emotionally Healthy Marriage: Growing Closer by Understanding One Another.* Revell of Baker Publishing Group.

marriage. In previous chapters, we shared how our past experiences have been entangled with painful experiences. Our declaration of reconnecting to God through Jesus Christ provided confidence that we're delivered in those pains. However, this new life with Christ is just the beginning of a journey for a transformation that God intended for us, which includes His continuous work in our hearts. Just like what Apostle Paul wrote in 2 Corinthians;

> *"Therefore, if anyone is in Christ, he is a new creature; the old things passed away; behold, new things have come."*
> (2 Corinthians 5:17, NASB1995)

A Bible commentary has noted that the word "therefore" here implies that the reason why Apostle Paul concluded that anyone is a new creature who's in Christ is about that stated in the previous verse - the change of views regarding the Redeemer to which he there refers, and which was so great as to constitute a change like a new creation [51]. So, the phrase, *"If anyone is in Christ,"* becoming true Christians undergo such a change in their views, feelings, and eventually volition. This is not an outward reformation of life and manners but an inward principle of grace by God[52]. It is not an improvement of old principles of nature but an implantation of new principles of grace and holiness - a new heart, spirit, light, and life. So, the implantation of a new principle, which is God's truth that once separated from us, takes a process called the sanctification process. The sanctification process is a moment-by-moment challenge and won't be complete until we leave this world and meet God.

---

[51] J Stoop, Barnes Notes on the Bible. *Bible Hub*. www.biblehub.com
[52] Gill's Exposition of the Entire Bible. *Bible Hub*. www.biblehub.com

The journey is about trusting God and walking according to the guidance of the Holy Spirit (Galatians 5:16).

Just like in our situation. I (Annie) have observed and witnessed Rey's uprightness, particularly in his former career in the US Navy. Growing up, he's been this kinda "good kid" despite his parents' separation or his dad's choices that negatively impacted their family. In one opportunity, he tried to teach our children about honesty (particularly in their school activities); he once shared that he received an A+ grade from one class during high school. He knew he failed the test so he approached the teacher after the class and reminding that it could have been a mistake. The next day, the teacher decided to retain his grade and commented on his honesty in front of the class. In many instances, he successfully said no to many bad things, which further strengthened his training in the military, and he has now realized and tested what motivated him on this good quality of his. His motivation was not to be like his father, so every winning moment that puts him in such a situation is like an affirmation that eventually builds confidence and pride. This time, living with Christ, a new life of being able to say "no" will be focused on submission to God's authority (alone), and it is only by His grace, mercy, and love.

Similarly, I (Rey) have noticed Annie's gifts and attitude in delivering quality work. Her challenges of not having "much" since childhood didn't hold her back from having a good education and career. Her initiative and hard work gave us the state award for being small business owners in the minority-owned category. The success is supposedly a testament to God's provision, but God was not firmly present in her (or even in our household) during such a season. Her "soft-pedaling" of Christianity was not strong enough in Satan's temptation, which led her to dwell on that success and take full credit for it. Now, in her renewed faith, that established confidence and pride will be replaced by dependence on God's grace, mercy, and love.

This is our battle. Our continuous battle to not fall into Satan's trap of dwelling on the sin of pride. Just like what Solomon shared in Proverbs 16:18, pride goes before destruction. This is what Satan wants for us, to dwell in such pride until it reaches destruction. This pride is a condition of losing the submission to God's authority, even for a brief moment or in the tiniest detail of our lives. It is this pride that allows Satan to traffic our BEPs (anger, fear, sadness, and shame), drive us to further vulnerability with deep anxiousness, and put blurriness on the message of the Gospel. Our emotions are part of God's creation to us. It was corrupted because of our former life distanced from God and the nature of sin in our flesh. Yet a new life with Him could turn these negative emotions into a constant remembrance that we need to be anchored in Christ and strengthened by the power of the Holy Spirit gifted to us. Our obedience to watch over our hearts with all diligence (Proverbs 4:23a) is not the consistent act of avoidance or disregarding those negative emotions. It is about understanding them and allowing God's transformation, which enables us to experience His grace and unity with the Holy Spirit. That is the flowing of the springs of life (Proverbs 4:23b), a heart sanctified by the grace of God.

May it be our constant reminder that the Christlikeness that God intends for us comes with a heart that He desires - exchanged by Him, empowered by Him, established by Him, and enriched by Him.

- Exchanged by Him
  - *"Moreover, **I will give you a new heart** and put a new spirit within you; and I will remove the heart of stone from your flesh and give you a heart of flesh."* (Ezekiel 36:26, NASB1995)

- Empowered by Him
  - *"**I will put My Spirit within you** and cause you to walk in My statutes, and you will be careful to observe My ordinances."* (Ezekiel 36:27, NASB1995)

- Established by Him
  - *"**You will live in the land that I gave to your forefathers**;"* (Ezekiel 36:28a, NASB1995)

- Enriched by Him
  - *"..so **you will be My people, and I will be your God**."* (Ezekiel 36:28b, NASB1995)

Understanding the nature of our hearts and how God desires for it, provided a certain layer of our connection to Him. We may be facing challenges but the understanding serves as a signification encouragement for our continuous journey in Christianity. As God continues to transform our hearts, we'll notice that we're no longer comfortable with sin. A simple act or even thinking about it, there's a strong conviction from the Holy Spirit that will remind us how such a sinful act could affect our fellowship with God. When we (Rey & Annie) encountered such a difficult season that almost shook our faith in God, He not only reminded us of the Gospel message but also some methods that continuously transform our minds and hearts.

CHAPTER 8
METHODS OF DUTY

The learning process about the "heart" requires a continuous discussion. It's not something that we can just simply take a course and project a comprehensive timeline, thinking that it will respond accordingly to any pain. While we're still here living on this earth, it will be our continuous process to guard our hearts and trust God's transformation process that He's doing on us. All of us are (have been or are in the process of being) wounded and will still encounter pain, whether believers or not. Sadly, bringing this wound to Christ is not always an appealing option despite the evident consequences that we're facing. We'd rather go in some options to numb the pain instead of dealing with it right away. Then, next thing we know, we're in the bondage of anesthetizing behaviors that could be helping us to get by, but in reality, it doesn't get us better. By the time we encounter some convictions along this life journey, the anesthetizing behaviors built in us are now contrasting with these convictions. Thus, we go back to what we usually do, and we'd wrongly use Apostle Paul's words in Romans 7:15 to try to balance our anesthetizing behavior and convictions. Dr. Jerry Root pointed this out in the C.S. Lewis Institute's study series *"The Screwtape Letters,"* and he noted;

> *"Our wounds are deeper than our convictions. And, if we're not finding the grace of God healing us in the places of our life, especially in the troth period, we become particularly susceptible to the sins of the flesh."* [53](Dr. Jerry Root)

Our wounds, whether emotional or psychological hurts, traumas, or adverse life experiences, can impact more of our behavior than our convictions. This is very evident, particularly when we're still in the process of critical healing under Christ. However, this doesn't necessarily mean that we no longer experience the possible complications of anesthetizing behavior and conviction once we (thought) passed such healing. If this is our perspective, then we're contrasting the complete sense of the sanctification process. The next thing we know that anesthetizing behavior becomes Satan's tool for us to commit and dwell in sin. Understanding those wounds and using them as an excuse to cover fears and insecurities is not pleasing to God. Also, understanding those wounds and not acting upon them (in a sense, delaying decisions or avoiding intentionality) is not pleasing to God. This just tells us how our genuine encounter and acceptance of the Gospel leads us to what Apostle Paul said in Philippians;

> *"So then, my beloved, just as you have always obeyed, not as in my presence only, but now much more in the absence, work out your salvation with fear and trembling."*
> (Philippians 2:12, NASB1995)

Our genuine encounter with the Gospel message leads us to exercise this salvation with "fear in trembling." It's not fear and trembling that torments misgiving but profound reverence for God. So, despite the given battle of weakness in the flesh, the brokenness of the world, and the existence of evil, we're pursuing this new life that takes serious attention to anything that will affect our fellowship with

---

[53] (Previous Page) Dr. Jerry Root, *"The Screwtape Letters with Dr. Jerry Root"*. C.S. Lewis Institute. www.cslewisinstitute.org

God - sin. If our former life doesn't give much attention to sin—including those traces of wickedness that follow from our thoughts to our hearts—then accepting Jesus Christ brings the Holy Spirit, which makes us uncomfortable with any sin that affects our relationship with God. He didn't let us move forward in this new life unequipped. Besides the modeling of Jesus Christ and the influence of the Holy Spirit, God left us a record of His words - the Bible. It is the lamp unto our feet and light to our path (Psalm 119:105). It is the best source that's God-breathed and is useful for teaching, rebuking, correcting, and training, so all of us, His servants, would be thoroughly adequate and equipped (2 Timothy 3:16-17).

We (Rey & Annie) could be more disastrous if we didn't discipline ourselves to be attached to the word of God. There have been days when we've been challenged to keep up with the reading schedule, but we've noticed how we are when we don't start our day by reflecting on God's words and taking some quiet time with Him. There were also some instances that it was difficult to obey, but God's profound promises and edification are powerfully speaking and urging for action. The Bible has become our great reference in every discussion, decision-making process, and even encouragement, particularly in challenging times. It is such a blessing that we have this reference amid the corrupted world and time that we live in today. The Bible is indeed a great source for understanding God's wisdom. It's our guide in living this life. As Joshua's encouragement (Joshua 1:8), the book of Law must be strictly and carefully observed - to read, mark, and inwardly digest it. Similarly how Matthew Henry summarized the wisdom shared by Solomon in Proverbs 4;

"When the things of God are to be taught precept must be upon precept, and line upon line, not only because the things themselves are of great worth and weight, but because men's minds, at the best, are unapt to admit them and commonly prejudiced against them; and therefore Solomon, in this chapter, with a great variety of expression and a pleasant powerful flood of divine eloquence, inculcates the same things that he had pressed upon us in the foregoing chapters (of Proverbs)." [54]*(Matthew Henry)*

Henry's comment echoes just what's noted in Isaiah 28:10, which suggests that spiritual teaching requires repetition and gradual building of concepts in us. It implies that understanding divine truths is not just a one-time event but a process of layering and reinforcing new ideas in our minds and hearts. It is not just a one-time understanding but a continuous revisiting of knowledge and concepts multiple times. Each time, there's an addition of more depth, complexity, or connections. Henry continued by acknowledging that God's truths are inherently valuable and significant, which tells us the need for careful and repeated teaching. He didn't opt in his comment about the human limitations in grasping spiritual concepts. He pointed out that even well-intentioned people may struggle to understand or accept these truths, which is an excellent reminder that we must pray first and ask for God's guidance when coming in God's words.

Even coming to God's words is a continuous process anchored in God's guidance. We must remember that we

---

have access to the Author, and He truly wants us to know, understand, and live a life paralleled in every word that comes from His mouth.

At first, Annie and I (Rey) struggle to connect when discussing our encounter in God's words. We have a different approach to studying the Bible. I got used to the practice of reading from Genesis to Revelations, and I haven't stopped the cycle since I started reading in 2018. On the other hand, Annie would love to take some time to read and dig deeper into every chapter. She likes checking commentaries and sometimes even refers to Hebrew or Greek translations. Yet, after the moment that God showed us a unified message in both of our reading habits (which we shared in Chapter 6), we always look forward to sharing what we have learned and how we can help each other, particularly in terms of accountability. It may have taken us some time, but the continuous process and commitment to journeying together under God's authority have helped us develop a spiritual habit beneficial to our relationship. Our different approaches have turned to complementing methods for both of us. We've collected many testimonies on how the things we've read and learned are coming alive in our journey. It is such a great affirmation to be anchored in His words. We don't know where we would be apart from His words. The struggles we have to go through and the tough decisions we need to make, we relied on His promises. When outcomes are beyond our expectations and limited understanding, God's words serve as our cane in every step we have to take. We both knew that God's presence was our greatest blessing (and will continue to be) and that we couldn't have a continual journey apart from His words. So, when dealing with the very dark season of our lives, we incline ourselves more in God's words. The Bible doesn't just give us suitable warnings not to do or incline in evil's ways, which is the strong temptation when facing trials or feeling deeply wounded in pain. The Bible has comprehensive records of knowledge and wisdom that could teach us how to do well despite rough roads. As Mathew Henry further comments in Proverbs 4,

> *"It is not enough for us to shun the occasions of sin, but we must study the methods of duty."* [55](Matthew Henry)

The battle with sin continues, but our relationship with Christ should not let us remain defeated. Our continuous learning process eliminates innocence and replaces it with understanding anchored in God. So, when we experienced the most challenging season of our lives that shook our family and our relationships with others, the struggle was there. This struggle involves substantial misunderstanding, confusion, doubt, and pain. We thought we were already firmly anchored in His words, but God let us go through an experience that tested our connection with His words. We were disconnected from many, and the situation left us with nothing but merely relying on God and His presence. The painful wound even tried to put blurriness and confusion when we try to come in His words. There were moments when we felt God's silence and Satan's attempt at deception were attempting to speak louder.

---

[55] Henry, M. (n.d.). Matthew Henry Commentary. *Blue Letter Bible.* https://www.blueletterbible.org

Such deception includes discouragement from our shortcomings, creating shame or fear, and directing those negative emotions to further disconnection with God instead of treating those negative emotions as God's reminder. This reminds us to hold tighter to God's words because those negative emotions could be God's way for us to experience the profound reality of His words.

In the previous chapter, we've shared how painful incidents or seasons significantly affect our journey with Jesus Christ. However, in Chapter 7, we devoted space to understanding the problem of pain, and such understanding drove us to the deep realization that God wants our hearts. With a similar incident, God showed us another layer of importance in anchoring our journey in His words, further diligence in guarding our hearts, putting away deceitful mouths, and our covenant with our "eyes." In finding ourselves in a situation with limited options or no options, don't let the language of discouragement that highlights shortcomings drive you to further complications. Instead, the reality of our shortcomings can be a way to a more intentional exercise of salvation. The following "methods of duty" didn't just help us survive this difficult season but also a relearning period of God's intent for us and our marriage.

Method of Duty 1 | Anchored in God's Words

*"20My son, give attention to **my words**;*

*Incline your ear to **my sayings**.*

21Do not let them depart from your sight;

Keep them amid your heart.

22For they are life to those who find them

And health to all their body.

(Proverbs 4:20-22, NASB1995)

The common reasons that we find ourselves engaged in God's words are either (1) to gain knowledge and (2) to find comfort in His powerful message. Both can be experienced through God's words, yet the encouragement for engagement in God's words is beyond a collection of knowledge or a "feel good" source. God wants us to heed His words by (a) *"Inclining our ears to His sayings."* The "inclination of ears" is not about passive listening but engaged and focused attention. Our attentive hearing of God's words indicates His grace working in our hearts and evident development and transformation. It's only by God's grace that we're able to receive His message in between those written words. We can also carry out the message we captured from those words through His grace. Carrying this out is not easy. That leads to the second way of paying attention to God's words: (b) *"Do not let these words depart from our sight."* We have to view and review them regularly; in everything, let's aim to conform. Our frequent readings and keeping in sight contribute to turning God's words into a rule and directory to steer the course of our lives. Our commitment to inclining our ears and keeping in sight will be challenging if we're not following the third way of engagement: (c) *"Keep His words in the midst of our heart."* We must ponder these words, meditate on them, and not forget them. We must show the most affectionate regard for God's words and consider them the most valuable treasure; the best place to keep them is in our hearts. The verse (Proverbs 4:22) explains why we must incline ourselves to God's words. **Reason 1,** *"Life to those who find them,"* is the means of spiritual life we could not live without; by faith, we can live upon it. **Reason 2,** *"And health to all their body,"* keeps our body and soul in good plight. The teachings and wisdom in the word of God can help us maintain our well-being. Our obedience to these teachings can bless us with balance, peace, and overall health.

Charles Spurgeon shared *(published via C.S. Lewis Institute)* a guideline to help us read God's words that will be profitable in our life journey.

Reading the Word of God Profitably by Charles Spurgeon [56]

- *Read the Bible with an earnest desire to understand it - (Do not be content to just read the words of Scripture. Seek to grasp the message they contain)*

- *Read the Scriptures with a simple, childlike faith and humility - (Believe what God reveals. Reason must bow to God's revelation.)*

- *Read the word with a Spirit of obedience and self-application - (Appy what God says to yourself and obey His will in all things.)*

- *Read the holy Scriptures every day - (We quickly lose the nourishment and strength of yesterday's bread. We must feed our souls daily upon the manna God has given us.)*

- *Read the whole Bible and read it in an orderly way - ("All Scripture is given by inspiration of God and is profitable" I know of no better way to read the Bible than to start at the beginning and read straight through to the end, a portion every day, comparing Scripture with Scripture.)*

---

[56] C.S. Lewis Institute. (2021). Reading the Word of God Profitably: by Charles Spurgeon. *Reading the Word of God Profitably.* https://www.cslewisinstitute.org/

- *Read the word of God fairly and honestly - (As a general rule, any passage of Scripture means what it appears to mean. Interpret every passage in this simple manner, in its context.)*
- *Read the Bible with Christ constantly in view - (The whole Bible is about Him. Look for Him on every page. He is there. If you fail to see Him there, you need to read the page again.)*

Spurgeon continued with this profound comment;

> *"There is no college for holy education like that of the blessed Spirit, for He is an ever-present tutor, to whom we have only to bend the knee, and He is at our side, the expositor of truth."*

It's only by God's grace could we be this inclined and engaged in His words. His words will not only enlighten us about the truths we weren't aware of, particularly in those days when we were separated from Him, but God will also let us experience the reality of His words. Indeed, it's a blessing when our intentional inclination to God's words is part of our commitment to the new life with Christ. There's also a different sense of God's blessings when a couple is united in navigating this life anchored in God's words. We can experience direct relations and unified God's message. Hearing and understanding our spouse's encounter through Words gives us a good perspective on how God transforms them. We got better approaches to attending to the roles that God entrusted us, and, by praying and supporting them intentionally, particularly when they faced their weak points and shortcomings. We will not experience the blessings of progression in our discussion as husband and wife apart from the profound guidance of God's words.

Method of Duty 2 | Watching diligently on the heart

[23]Watch over your heart with all diligence,

For from it flow the springs of life.

(Proverbs 4:23, NASB1995)

The previous chapter (Chapter 7) detailed our discovered truths and learning experiences on how great diligence is needed since our hearts are naturally deceitful and treacherous. Keeping a strict eye is not about merely in the context of being critical but replacing any harmful factors with a constant reminder of Christ for His grace as well as the Holy Spirit's continuous work of transformation. [57]Matthew Henry shared a good list of how we can diligently watch over our hearts;

- *Keep our hearts from doing hurt and getting hurt*
- *Keep our hearts from defiled by sin and disturbed by trouble*
- *Keep our hearts as jewels, as our vineyards*
- *Keep a conscience void of offense (by maintaining a clear conscience free from feelings of guilt, regret, or offense towards oneself or others; act in a manner that is honest, ethical, and upright, leading to a sense of inner peace and integrity)*
- *Keep out bad thoughts and keep up good thoughts*
- *Keep the affections upon right objects and due in bounds*

Learning this "heart" thing and reviewing every practical point Henry shared might discourage us as we see

---

[57] Henry, M. (n.d.). Matthew Henry Commentary. *Blue Letter Bible.* https://www.blueletterbible.org

Learning this "heart" thing and reviewing every practical point Henry shared might discourage us as we see how far we are. Yet, reflecting on the reason specified in Proverbs 4:23, *"for from it flow the springs of life,"* we could get encouragement because of God's grace. Our relationship with Christ will not let us view our shortcomings as a factor for passiveness but as a hopeful journey. We could look forward to the journey of God's sanctification process with excitement about the intimacy we will experience with Him along the way. Our (Rey & Annie) journey in this "heart matter" has led us to many instances of pain. We've experienced receiving the offense and being an object of offense, not just between us as husband and wife, but also towards our children and others. Only by God's grace can we be intentional about it or given opportunities to be purposeful for it. We're thankful for every opportunity that God allowed us to be controlled by Him or be surrounded by fellow believers who gave us space to journey alongside them despite rough patches. Our continuous journey to this matter has led us to understand and give importance to self-awareness. Our intent approach is not just a discussion of pain but also an admission of the struggles of making a choice not to be Satan's object of this pain. Situations like this helped us view and experience how profoundly significant it is to journey Christianity authentically. It's not about making a good performance checklist but the honest admission of our weak points where we rely strongly on God's help and guidance.

Method of Duty 3 | Putting away a deceitful mouth

²⁴*Put away from you a **deceitful mouth***
And put devious speech far from you.

(Proverbs 4:24, NASB1995)

"Our hearts being naturally corrupt, out of them a great deal of corrupt communication," [58]Henry noted. Considering the weakness of our flesh and inconsistent watchfulness, we may see ourselves fall into the temptation of evil words such as cursing, swearing, lying, slandering, brawling, filthiness, and foolish talking. We're quick to directly relate "deceitful mouth" and "devious speech" into swearing alone, wherein the Biblical description goes a little deeper. In some Bible translations, *"deceitful mouth and devious speech"* is translated as *"perverseness of mouth and waywardness of lips."* [59]"Perversity of mouth" is fraudulent, deceitful speech that twists, distorts, perverts, or misrepresents what is true and false (Proverbs 4:24, Proverbs 6:12, Proverbs 19:1). While the "waywardness of lips" means speech which turns aside from what is true and right. Our attentiveness in our hearts translates into attentiveness over our mouths (Matthew 12:34), and as most experts noted, our speech is the index of our mind. Understanding Biblical terms isn't just an addition of knowledge but an opportunity to add a layer of seriousness to God's words, particularly His commands.

Similarly, in the word *"lying,"* our common conception is distorted truth alone. Yet, in the wisdom shared in Proverbs 6:16-19, *"The six things that the Lord hates,"* it is noticeable how "lying / lies" were used in the two separate factors despite a common understanding that it denotes a singular meaning.

---

[58] Henry, M. (n.d.). Matthew Henry Commentary. *Blue Letter Bible.* https://www.blueletterbible.org

[59] Pulpit Commentary. *Bible Hub.* https://www.biblehub.com

The usage of the words completes the thought intent for understanding. Like the "lying tongue" noted in Proverbs 6:17 means speaking falsehood, knowingly and willingly, to deceive others, such as hurting someone's character or even flattering a friend.[60] On the other hand, the phrase, *"A false witness who utters lies,"* in Proverbs 6:19 means the sin of bearing false witness against someone.[61] The complete meaning is supported in the other half of the verse, *"And one who spreads strife among brothers,"* which means spreading words that will further create disagreement.

We may think that this primarily applies to our relationships with others. Yet, if we could give ourselves some time to reflect on ourselves (married individuals), we can remember instances when we spoke to our spouse that fell on any defined terms above. Thank God that we have Jesus Christ, who paid for our sins and gave us hope to be delivered from the bondage of this sin.

Method of Duty 4 | Covenant with our eyes

[25]*Let your eyes look directly ahead*

And let your gaze be fixed straight in front of you.

(Proverbs 4:25, NASB1995)

May we focus on the path of God's truth and righteousness without turning or looking to the right or left. Our "eyes" attention and focus on Jesus Christ, who is the author, finisher of our faith, and our source of grace. May our attention not be attracted to the vanity of this world. Vanity, futile, and futility come from the Hebrew word "hebel." Hebel appears more in Ecclesiastes than in any

---

[60-61] Henry, M. (n.d.). Matthew Henry Commentary. *Blue Letter Bible.* https://www.blueletterbible.org

Vanity, futile, and futility come from the Hebrew word "hebel." Hebel appears more in Ecclesiastes than in any other book of the Bible. Primarily, it means breath, vapor, and light wind.

Experts shared that it denotes what [62];

- Passes away more or wholly and quickly (like no depth)
- Leaves either no result or no adequate result behind
- Fails to satisfy the mind of man, which naturally craves something permanent and progressive
- Turn to be man's idol that replaces God's position in hearts and minds

We've seen how the serpent successfully put the deceptiveness in place and supported by the looks of the forbidden fruit - "delight" and "desirable" (Genesis 3:6). It was pleasant to the eyes and very inviting to the taste. Similarly, in our lives today, if we're not grounded in God's authority, we'll quickly get distracted and fall on the things that look delightful and desirable. Yet these things, chances, or even relationships do not align with God's design, purpose, and will for us.

We tend to equate this matter in terms of adultery, where one married individual falls into the temptation of a desirable "other" individual. In reality, it's those small instances that are part of our daily living that establish our behavior of delighting in temporal things in this world. We'll just realize how deep we're already sinking in when we start to experience its effect on other aspects of our

---

[62] Barnes' Notes on the Bible. Bible Hub. https://www.biblehub.com

marriage. I (Annie) realized how much stuff we have in our house when I couldn't find a proper place for the things I bought inspired by my Pinterest boards or collections from TikTok videos. Instead of taking such valuable time to organize further and manage our financial records, I consumed so much time browsing social media channels and training myself to be delighted and desired on the things that are no longer needed. Indeed the "covenant with our eyes," is a very subtle behavior, and we will just realize how enslaved we are when we're facing the consequences of those small actions that were collected over time.

Method of Duty 5 | Act considerately in all we do

[26]*Watch the path of your feet*

And all your ways will be established.

(Proverbs 4:26, NASB1995)

Consider well what path it is, whether right or wrong. If our reference to examining our paths is apart from God, we could lead ourselves on a journey that's not "established." We have a sincere heart and actions to plan our ways, but the Lord is the only One who truly establishes our steps (Proverbs 16:9). Matthew Henry made a very profound comment;

> *"We must consider our past ways and examine what we have done, and our present ways, what we are doing, whither we are going, and see that we walk circumspectly."* [63](Matthew Henry)

---

[63] Henry, M. (n.d.). Matthew Henry Commentary. Blue Letter Bible. https://www.blueletterbible.org

Henry points out the importance of self-reflection and self-examination. We should reflect on our past actions and behaviors and evaluate our current actions and decisions. It's not about being critical in a negative sense but about walking this life journey mindfully and attentively. This encourages us to be intentional in our actions, which helps us stay on the right path and avoid any potential pitfalls or further consequences in this life.

Rey & Annie's Regular Devotional Time

It is about actively shaping our paths and understanding our journey - (1) reflecting on the past to learn from it, (2) being mindful of our present actions, and (3) considering the future implications of our choices. These practical applications will surely be helpful when we align our self-reflection and self-examination with the grace, mercy, and love of God.

Annie and I (Rey) may have established a good habit of discussion when we're processing situations or decisions.

Although those justifications and logical reasonings were in parallel to our behaviors and perspectives that were developed and shaped when we weren't anchored in Jesus Christ. Because of our limited knowledge of God's attributes and inexperience of His presence in life, we've established "steps" in our life journey apart from God's design, will, and purpose. It wasn't an easy journey to replace these old behaviors and perspectives when we decided to accept Jesus Christ in our lives and renew our faith intentionally. We realized how our actions were impacted because we don't know God, personally - in a relationship. We didn't realize that knowing Him is not just by books or knowledge, but by experiences so our growing faith is not just reflected in traditions and cultures. Rather a living faith that encourages us to move forward and submit to the sanctification process that He intends for us. There were many instances that our focus was tested, and even to this day, Satan's temptation for us to dwell on those behaviors is like a roaring lion waiting to devour. In very vulnerable instances we find ourselves, we remind ourselves that we're on a journey with God, and we take time to reflect on His character and attributes. Josh McDowell released a list entitled, *"Discover God's Character: 13 Key Attributes of God,"*[64] that summarized God's characters and attributes. The list helps us to go over the associated verses, so we can find encouragement and guidance whenever we're facing difficult situations that require intimate and intentional self-reflection. Thus leading us to change our actions - actions that are anchored in God's character.

---

[64] McDowell, J. (2020). Discover God's Character: 13 Key Attributes of God. *Discover God's Attributes.* https://www.josh.org/

God's 13 Key Attribute[65]	Notes
1. God is a Personal Spirit	• *God is infinite* • *God is self-existent* • *God is eternal* • *God is self-sufficient* • *Psalm 143:6, Jeremiahs 29:13*
2. God is All-Powerful	• *God has the power to create anything from nothing (Psalm33:6-9)* • *God has power to deliver (Exodus 13:3)* • *God's creative power is beyond our comprehension (Job 38:1-11)* • *His resurrection power is immeasurably great (Ephesians 1:19-20)* • *His creation reflects His power (Psalm 19:1-4)* • *His powerful word sustains everything (Hebrews 1:3)* • *He has power over death (Revelation 1:18)* • *No one can challenge what God does (Daniel 4:35)*

	• *Reveals Himself as the almighty God (Genesis 17:1)*
3. God is Present Everywhere	• *All creation is dependent upon His presence (Colossians 1:17)* • *God's continual presence brings contentment (Hebrews 13:5)* • *God is everywhere and no one can escape Him (Psalm 139:7-12)* • *No task is too large or too difficult for Him (Jeremiah 32:17,27)* • *One cannot hide from God (Jeremiah 23:23-24)*
4. God Knows Everything	• *Daniel 2:21, Psalm 139:1-6, Jeremiah 29:11, James 1:5-7*
5. God is Sovereign	• *God controls time and seasons (Daniel 2:21)* • *God powerfully delivered His people from Egypt (Exodus 12:29-32; 13:13-31)* • *God has dominion over the affairs of people (Job 12:13-25)* • *God controls nature for His purposes (Job 37:2-13)* • *God chose His people to become like Christ (Romans 8:28-30)* • *God chose His people before He made the world (Ephesians 1:4)*

	• *God's eternal purpose is to make His wisdom known (Ephesians 3:10-11)* • *He raises and removes rulers (Daniel 2:21)* • *He has a plan for His people and will carry it out (Ephesians 1:5,11)* • *He chose His people to save and purify them (2 Thessalonians 2:13)* • *He is the only Sovereign (1 Timothy 1:17, 6:15)* • *The Creator looks after His creation (Psalm 104:3-32)* • *The powerful Creator reduces human rulers to nothing (Isaiah 40:21-26)* • *Relationship with God requires worship (John 4:24)*
6. God is Holy	• *God guards His holy reputation (Ezekiel 36:21-23)* • *God's holiness demands exclusive worship (Josh 24:19)* • *He disciplines believers to impart His holiness to them (Hebrews 12:10)* • *His holiness is unique (Exodus 15:11)* • *His holiness is the standard for believers' behavior (Leviticus 19:2, 1 Peter 1:15-16)* • *His holy presence rejects impurity (Isaiah 6:3-5)*

	• *No one else is holy like He is (1 Samuel 2:2)* • *The most holy One deserves constraint honor (Revelation 4:8)*
7. God is the Absolute Truth	• *Believers know that God is true (John 3:33)* • *Eternal life is knowing the only true God (John 17:3)* • *Even if all humanity lies, God remains true (Romans 3:4)* • *God is truth (John 14:6)* • *God follows through on His promises (Numbers 11:22-2; 31-34)* • *God's words are true and completely righteous (Psalm 19:9)* • *God's truth is everlasting (Psalm 117:2)* • *God's word is truth (John 17:17)* • *God's words are faithful and true (Revelation 21:5; 22:6)* • *God's truth can be suppressed to our peril (Romans 1:18)* • *He is "the God of truth" (Pslam 31:5; Isaiah 65:16)* • *God doesn't lie but keeps His word (Numbers 23:19)* • *He is full of grace and truth (John 1:14)* • *His Spirit guides believers into all truth (John 16:13)*

	• *The Holy Spirit is characterized by truth in every way (John 14:17; 15:26; 1 John 5:6)* • *True freedom comes from abiding in God's truth (John 8:31-32)*
8. God is Righteous	• *His righteousness is absolute (Psalm 71:19)* • *He rules out of righteousness (Psalm 97:2)* • *He is righteous in everything He does (Psalm 145:17)* • *He delights in demonstrating righteousness (Jeremiah 9:24)* • *In the end, the righteous Judge will judge righteously (2 Timothy 4:8)* • *People must declare humbly that God alone is righteous (Exodus 9:27, 2 Chronicles 12:6)*
9. God is Just	• *A day is fixed for His righteous judgment of the world (Acts 17:31)* • *All sin is ultimately against a righteous God (Psalm 51:4)* • *All God's ways are righteous and deserve praise (Revelations 15:3)* • *God alone is the judge (James 4:12)* • *God judges all people with justice (Psalm 9:7-8)*

	• *God's law and judgments are completely righteous (Psalm 19:7-9)* • *He exercises justice toward all humanity (Genesis 18:25)* • *He is just in all His ways (Deuteronomy 32:4)* • *God rightly judges heart, mind, and deeds (Jeremiah 17:10)* • *Jesus pleads our case (1 John 2:1)* • *The Messiah will judge all with complete justice (Isaiah 11:4-5)* • *The righteous Messiah will establish a righteous people (Jeremiah 33:16)* • *The righteous God justifies those who believe in Jesus (Romans 3:25-26)*
10. God is Love	• *As a father, God corrects His beloved children (Proverbs 3:12)* • *Believers should imitate God's universal love (Matthew 5:44-45)* • *Eternal plans are motivated by His love (Ephesians 1:4-5)* • *God loves and preserves His godly people (Psalm 37:28)* • *God loves His people, even when they are faithless (Hosea 3:1)* • *God deserves thanks because of His perpetual love (Psalm 100:5)* • *God loved the word enough to send His Son to die (John 3:16)*

	• *God loves those who love His son (and obey Him) (John 14:21)* • *His love is poured into believers' hearts (Romans 5:5)* • *God is love, and those who know God love others (1 John 4:7-8; 20-21)*
11. God is Merciful	• *God will never relent from showing mercy to His children (Psalm 23:6)* • *God will listen to our pleas for mercy (Psalm 30:8)* • *Because of mercy, god washes away our transgressions (Psalm 51:1)* • *Because God is merciful, He has not hidden Himself from us (Psalm 69:16)* • *Mercy comes to those who confess their sins (Proverbs 28:13)* • *Mercy is given to those who are themselves merciful (Matthew 5:7)* • *God desires to show mercy to His people instead of having His people try to obtain their righteousness (Matthew 9:13)* • *God shows mercy to those who fear His name (Luke 1:50)* • *Our mercy of others should be an imitation of God's mercy to us (Luke 6:36)* • *Knowing God's mercy encourages us to follow Him (Romans 12:1).*

12. God is Faithful	• God forgives to repentant (1 John 1:9) • God is faithful to the faithful (Deuteronomy 7:7-11) • God deserves thanks for His constant faithfulness (Psalm 100:5) • God is faithful through calamity (Lamentations 3:22-23) • God faithfully matures believers (2 Thessalonians 5:24) • God is faithful to fulfill His promises (Hebrews 10:23) • His faithfulness endures (Psalm 119:90) • His faithfulness is immeasurable (Psalm 36:5)
13. God Never Changes	• God never changes (Malachi 3:6) • God is consistent throughout all time (Hebrews 13:8) • God is good - all the time (James 1:17) • He doesn't lie and is true to His word (numbers 23:19) • His love is never-ending (Lamentations 3:22-23) • Though the universe will change, God never will (Psalm 102:25-27l Hebrews 1:10-12)

---

[65] McDowell, J. (2020). Discover God's Character: 13 Key Attributes of God. *Discover God's Attributes.* https://www.josh.org/

Method of Duty 6 | Act with steadiness, caution, and consistent

²⁷ *Do not turn to the right nor the left;*

Turn your foot from evil."

(Proverbs 4:27, NASB1995)

Although this verse shows a direct relation to verse 26, it is parallel to verse 25, which tells how our gaze should be concentrated. For verse 27, we're encouraged to have our "feet" not to deflect by either side, right or left. Keep our walks in this life on a straight path, upright. Refrain from any "side" steps that tempt us to do evil things or dwell in sin, rather walk faithfully under God's authority. Jesus Christ taught us to pray, *"And do not lead us into temptation, but deliver us from evil,"* (Matthew 6:11). If we genuinely ask God to lead us and not fall into temptation, then we should not be willingly going or leading ourselves to exposure of temptation.

Annie and I (Rey) have seen and read Proverbs numerous times but the message in chapter 4 strongly spoke to us during our difficult season. The message truly humbled and convicted us. We praise God that even on the edge and surrounded by failures and temptations, His presence is there to remind us not to dwell in sin. It wasn't an easy encounter particularly when we're facing the reality of our limited understanding and incidents beyond our control. Yet the greatness of God provides comfort despite being in a vulnerable situation that tends to afloat the weakness of our flesh. The wisdom shared by Solomon in the Old Testament may not directly specify God's grace or even the name of Jesus Christ. Yet those commands that we know we've fallen short in big time speak loudly about how blessed all of us are today for having God's grace. The more we have a long list of our shortcomings, the more important that we should have Christ in our lives. However, our journey with Christ doesn't equate to continuous ignorance of a life that God intends for us. So our understanding of the "methods of duty," is the continuous process of replacing our old perspective and actions that once lived apart from God. It's not a set of standards or checklist, but a guide towards a life depending on God's guidance and presence. This is the beauty of seeking an understanding through God's wisdom. We're equipping ourselves in the continuous battle of choosing Jesus Christ against the weakness of our flesh, the brokenness of this world, and the existence of evil.

"For our struggle is not against flesh and blood, but against the rulers, against the powers, against the world focus of this darkness, against the spiritual forces of wickedness in the heavenly places. Therefore, take up the full armor of God, so that you will be able to resist the evil day and, having done everything, to stand firm. Stand firm therefore, HAVING GIRDED YOUR LOINS WITH TRUTH, and HAVING PUT ON THE BREASTPLATE OF RIGHTEOUSNESS, and having shod YOUR FEET WITH THE PREPARATION OF THE GOSPEL OF PEACE; in addition to all, taking up the shield of faith with which you will be able to extinguish all the flaming arrows of the evil one. And take THE HELMET OF SALVATION, and the sword of the Spirit, which is the word of God. With all prayer and petition, pray at all times in the Spirit, and with this in view, be on the alert with all perseverance and petition for all the saints," (Ephesians 6:13-18, NASB1995

CHAPTER 9
THE COUPLE'S JOURNEY

As we go deeper into the understanding of God and Christianity, the more we find sins of ourselves and far distant from His standard. Yet, this undeniable truth is leading us on the great blessing of His grace through Jesus Christ and the message of the cross. Maybe God intends to have four accounts of the Gospel (Matthew, Mark, John, and Luke) so we'll deeply understand its message and its great importance in today's life. Even God's consideration of the different personalities and giftedness of these authors allows us to further relate to how they delivered the story.

Matthew, also called Levi (Mark 2:14, Luke 5:27), was the son of Alphaneus (Luke 5:27). He is a tax collector and because of this job, many have considered him as the most qualified to take account of life and works of Jesus Christ[66]. In the very first verse of Matthew's account, his purpose is clear - to show that Jesus was the long-awaited King, the son of David, the Messiah whose arrival was prophesied in the Old Testament[67]. On the other hand, Mark, also known as John Mark, wrote a fast-paced Gospel that emphasizes Jesus' works rather than His teachings[68].

[66.] The Gospel of Matthew. *Blue Letter Bible.* https://www.blueletterbible.org

[67.] *The New Inductive Study Bible.* (2000). Precept Ministries International. Harvest House Publishers. www.harvestpublishers.com

[68.] *The New Inductive Study Bible.* (2000). Precept Ministries International. Harvest House Publishers. www.harvestpublishers.com

Mark shows Jesus' power and authority through the works He does as He obeys God, the Father. Mark's writings show Jesus came not to be served but to serve, and to give His life as a ransom to many. The third account of the Gospel is by Luke, known as the beloved physician (Colossians 4:14). Experts mentioned that Luke's writing of the Gospel shows several differences from the other Synoptic Gospels such as it's the only one to have a sequel which is the Acts of the Apostles[69]. We can see his companionship with Paul in 2 Timothy 4:11 and Philemon 1:24. The Gospel of Matthew recorded Jesus as King of the Jews, in Gospel of Mark as the Servant who gave His life, then Luke's writings demonstrated the carefulness of a historian with specification "in consecutive order."[70] Luke's purpose in writing is clearly stated in Luke 1:1-4, where he specified, *"...having investigated carefully from the beginning to write it out for you in consecutive order, most excellent Theophilus; so that you may know the exact truth about the things you have been taught."*

The fourth and final account of the Gospel was John's answer to God's call for writing and explained that Jesus came to reveal God, the Father (A.D. 85)[71]. John has been known as an eyewitness of Jesus' ministry (John 1:14, 19:35, 21:24). Besides the recorded history in the Bible, we're blessed today to have a good illustration of John's journey through the series "The Chosen."[72]

[69.] The Gospel of Luke. *Blue Letter Bible.* https://www.blueletterbible.org

[70-71.] *The New Inductive Study Bible.* (2000). Precept Ministries International. Harvest House Publishers. www.harvestpublishers.com

[72.] *Jenkins, D., Swanson, R., Thompson, T. (Writers). Jenkins, D. (Director). (Sep 2021). Thunder (Season 2, Episode 1) [The Chosen]. In Jenkins, D. (Executive Producer). The Chosen. Loaves & Fishes Production.*

It was in Season 2, Episode 1 where Jesus called John and his brother James, accompanied by their father Zebedee, while preparing the nets in the boat. Both brothers left the boat and their father to follow Jesus Christ (Matthew 4:18-22). Not only John is counted as among the inner circle of disciples (John 13:23-24, 20:2-10, 21:2,7,20), but he also refers to himself as the disciple whom Jesus loved (John 13:23, 20:2, 21:7, 20). John specifically states his purpose in the Gospel writings in John 20:31, *"but these have been written so that you may believe that Jesus is the Christ, the Son of God; and the believing you may have life in His name."* Therefore John's purpose for his Gospel writings is to confirm and secure Christians in faith.

We tend to look at these Gospel writings as recorded incidents from different angles. Yet, as we go further in understanding the purposes of the authors, it added more substance to the stated stories. Thus, we see the great interrelation of these four accounts. We got the opportunity to look deeper into these four accounts of the Gospel when we were facing a difficult season that shook our partnership as a couple, as parents, and even volunteered partners in sharing Jesus Christ with others. During the grieving days, we're holding on to the promises of God through the resurrection of Jesus Christ. It was also the message of the cross that encouraged us to finally end the grieving and seek God for our future steps. We're reminded of God's amazing grace through the story of Mary Magdalene during the resurrection story.

When Matthew took an account of the resurrection story, he started Matthew 28 at the time when the women made an early visit to Christ's tomb. He detailed the experience of the women that Jesus Christ was no longer there. Yet in the

Gospel account of Mark, he indicated in Mark 16:9 that Jesus Christ first showed up to Mary Magdalene, a woman who was saved from seven demons. Her healing made a story, but the observance of her consistent devotion to Jesus Christ truly solidified her deliverance from such a past life. She was there when Jesus Christ was crucified (John 19:25) and burial (Mark 15:47). She was among those who prepared the materials to embalm Jesus Christ (Mark 16:1). Most importantly, how can we forget the profound conversation she had with Jesus Christ detailed in John 20:11-18. Despite her expression of grief, doubt, and deep concern in John 20:13-15, she obeyed Christ to inform the rest about the resurrection. An action that proves Mary Magdalene is no longer seeking a "dead Jesus Christ" (John 20:15).

> [11]*But Mary was standing outside the tomb weeping; and so, as she wept, she stooped and looked into the tomb;* [12] *and she *saw two angels in white sitting, one at the head and one at the feet, where the body of Jesus had been lying.* [13] *And they *said to her, "Woman, why are you weeping?" She *said to them, "Because they have taken away my Lord, and I do not know where they have laid Him."* [14] *When she had said this, she turned around and *saw Jesus standing there, and did not know that it was Jesus.* [15] *Jesus *said to her, "Woman, why are you weeping? Whom are you seeking?" Supposing Him to be the gardener, she *said to Him, "Sir, if you have carried Him away, tell me where you have laid Him, and I will take Him away."* [16] *Jesus *said to her, "Mary!" She turned and *said to Him in Hebrew, "Rabboni!" (which means, Teacher).* [17] *Jesus *said to her, "Stop clinging to Me, for I have not yet ascended to the Father; but go to My brethren and say to them, 'I ascend to My Father and your Father, and My God and your God.' "*

18 Mary Magdalene *came, announcing to the disciples, "I have seen the Lord," and that He had said these things to her. (John 20: 11-18, NASB 1995)

Jesus Christ used her to inform the disciples and others about His resurrection. We saw how gracious He was with her that despite a quick episode of behaviors that somehow displayed doubt or uncertainties, Jesus still used her. Instead of looking for others who may have better responses, He still gave Mary instructions on what needed to get done at that moment. This particular account of John not only gave us a confirmation that our relationship with Christ can exist, but it does secured that life with Christ *(the life journey of Christianity)* is in the great foundation of His grace, mercy, and love.

There could be instances in our lives where the "battle" is so strong that we're being pushed to the edge leading to the display of behaviors. Such behaviors don't align with or support our relationship with Christ. God allows such so we can learn and have the opportunity to experience the strength He provides to overcome the temptation to dwell on such behavior (1 Corinthians 10:13). It's not about acting because we're capable of doing so, but actions that depend on the influence and power of the Holy Spirit. We're not able to experience God's reality in our lives if we keep avoiding instances or move forward without God for learning opportunities that involve our limited understanding and reality of our shortcomings. Instances like this define how anchored we are in the message of the Gospel.

Restore

When Annie and I (Rey) encounter some difficult "bumps," one of us will surely take the initiative to keep ourselves grounded and be reminded of God's sovereignty and all-knowing power. Yet when an incident left both of us heavily burdened with so many questions and confusion, we're left nothing but to come together in the foot of Jesus Christ. Moments like this bring our burdened hearts into gratefulness because it's the Gospel that's able to bring us back into fellowship with God. It's the Gospel that continues to unite us in whatever season we have to go through. It's only through Christ that we're restored - individually and as a couple.

The gift of restoration is not just a one-time episode but it's a continuing process of living anchored in Christ. Here's the common misconception of restoration. We thought that it was a one-time big deal and that we could easily and freely create guidelines and standards that follow our somewhat definition of "restored." Little did we know that how we view and understand "restoration from God," defines how we view our circumstances and even other people that surround us, particularly our spouse. The New American Standard Bible (NASB), Bible translation, has used the term "restore" 116 times. Those 116 usages of terms were from 21 Hebrew-Aramaic words which show the term "restore" associated with other various terms such as - *Raise (to arise, rise); Rebuild; Receive (favorably); Recover; Renew (Repair); Repay (Recompense, Reward); Replace; Restore to health; Restored (to be justified); Retraced; Return; Revive; Review* [73]. Although we know that the general concept of restoration in God through Jesus Christ is turning from sin and returning to God. Thus, resulting in restored relationships like marriage or restored identity as His child.

[73.] Lockman Foundation. (2001-2016). Bible Questions. https://bible.lockman.org/

Yet looking at those mentioned related terms we can conclude that restoration can't happen overnight. As observed, it's often our anxiousness for urgent rescue that affects the real process of restoration. We all desire to have a restored marriage - not just in the vision of this world but a healthy marriage that's anchored in God. Yet sometimes, this noble desire turns out to be our main focal point that we're missing the ultimate source of restored marriage - God. We're falling into the temptation of creating our standards to the point that we've been legalistic in our marriage. When Rey accepted Jesus and I (Annie) witnessed God's works in him, I became critical of his roles to the point that I failed to offer understanding and that moment became Satan's playground for our numerous conflicts. My focus should remain on God and His continuous restoration of us.

Just like what Annie has said, I (Rey) too became critical of her. Our sincere desire for accountability can easily fall into the evil's tricky design to be critical and legalistic. It is indeed a continuous journey of anchoring ourselves in God's grace so that even in accountability our focus remains on glorifying and praising God. Understanding that restoration is a continuous process is not putting less importance on our first encounter with God. Rather, that very first encounter, where we accepted Jesus Christ and experienced the baptism of the Holy Spirit, is equally important in our daily living as we undergo God's transformation of restoration. I (Rey) would always remind Annie and our children not to forget that "first encounter with God" moment. It will be significant in this life journey as God's message is consistent from the beginning. In whatever season or life circumstances we find and accept Jesus Christ should be our foundational story as we continue to journey this life with Him - because He is the same yesterday, today, and tomorrow (Hebrews 13:8).

Relearn

The consistency of acknowledging and choosing Jesus Christ doesn't directly equate to defining a certain standard or life status that we need to achieve as His followers. Rather, this consistency is the foundational truth that we carry as we move forward on this life journey of Christianity which is a continuous relearning. We have God's words (the Bible) as one of our great sources for this relearning, and our experiential learnings are also equally important and significant to our journey. This journey can't be apart from Jesus Christ. As He said in Matthew 11:29, " Take My yoke upon you and learn from Me," He invites us to learn from and through Him. Jesus, Himself, modeled to us the lifelong task of learning. At Jesus' young age, He was sitting among scholars in the temple, "..sitting in the midst of the teachers, both listening to them and asking them questions" (Luke 2:46). In the height of His ministry works and numerous teachings of parables, His words were clear in telling His disciples to learn a lesson from the fig tree (Matthew 24:32). Finally, to the point of His sufferings, there are learnings through obedience from the things He suffered (Hebrew 5:8). Looking at these pointers of His example regarding learning, it solidifies His command about discipleship. In the Bible, the fundamental meaning of the Greek word for disciple is "a learner." Thus, this tells us that discipleship is a lifelong learning process. This learning process is living a life that's anchored in Jesus Christ.

Rev. Edmund Chan shared how discipleship has become regimental instead of a redemptive journey with Jesus Christ. He shared the difference between regimental and redemptive journeys, and from these pointers, we can have a good self-evaluation of how we understand discipleship.

Discipleship as **Regimental** [74]	Discipleship as **Redemptive** [75]
• *Our performance* • *Our work* • *What we must do* • *Requirements and the law*	• *Our pilgrimage* • *Our walk with God* • *What God has done* • *Not the requirements but redemption of grace* • *It's a love of God*

The series has encouraged us to reevaluate ourselves and look deeper into our experience in discipleship. The timing of finding such has not only allowed us to understand discipleship better but also to realize the great blessing of how our marital relationship turned into discipleship - a couple united under the redemptive journey with Jesus Christ. Since then, our regular sharing of devotion is not just a run-down checklist of "I-will" statements, but a constant reflection on how we encountered Christ in every given time.

From "Restore" and "Relearn," we can see the obvious continual journey of Christian living. It may have taken us some time to realize this, as well as, experience the great blessing of intentionally adapting discipleship in our marriage. Yet the whole journey of discovery, taking actions and now sharing (through this book), have added layers of

---

[74-75] Chan, E.. (2024). *Series: Starting Over* . IDMC Movement. www.idmcmovement.com

learning and experiencing God. We're still facing challenges as God continues to transform us, but as we commit ourselves to moving forward, we're witnessing God's flowing grace, mercy, and love. One another important thing that we've learned, which is very significant in this journey with Christ, is our attention and commitment to continuously growing in humility. Thomas A. Tarrants mentioned in one of his articles;

> *"Pride is a universal human problem. Everyone suffers from it to some degree. When we have exalted ourselves in pride, God does not want to punish us and bring us low but rather to forgive and restore us."* (Thomas A. Tarrants, "Pride and Humility")[76]

In our (Rey & Annie) experiences, the disconnection with God has established prideful behavior in every survival and accomplishment we encountered while we lived a life away from His authority. Even in understanding and going deeper into our hearts, our BEPs (Basic Emotional Postures), which we mentioned in Chapter 7, weren't just a "pot" of pain that's waiting for moments to spill but also flavored with very subtle (yet dangerous) pride. God did a lot of humbling experiences before we open our hearts to the genuine realization (Chapter 1), and respond accordingly to His call (Chapter 2). Our initial learning of Christianity as a lifestyle - from knowing His design (Chapter 3) and intentionality to discipleship (Chapter 4), profoundly speaks to us that humility starts in submission to God's authority. This continuous humbling journey includes our

---

[76]Tarrants, T. III (2011).*Knowing & Doing: Pride and Humility.* C.S. Lewis Institute. https://www.cslewisinstitute.org/

dependence on Him against spiritual warfare (Chapter 5), the unity of our marriage under His banner (Chapter 6), the continuous guarding of our hearts (Chapter 7), and that we're no longer comfortable dwelling on sin (Chapter 8). It is indeed a growing journey that requires humility, and it starts in submission under Christ's kingship in our lives because it's only through Him that we can find genuine humility.

When William L. Kynes shared a teaching about *"Growing in Humility,"* he mentioned the common misconception of humility.

Humility is Not; [77]

- *False modesty (constantly downplaying your role; diminishing your contribution or gifts)*

- *Low self-esteem*

- *Intellectual doubt (constant self-doubt or lack of confidence in knowledge)*

- *Thinking poorly about yourself (humility is not thinking of yourself at all)*

Considering pride is a universal human problem, the reality is there's an added problem of humility misconception. Sadly, this misconception is not just observed among unbelievers, there's still a misconception among us, the believers. Not until we genuinely experience the message of the gospel, the reality of God in our lives, and the power of the Holy Spirit, we will strongly be tempted by this misconception of humility. Kynes pointed out that humility is nothing but the truth.

---

[77] Kynes, W.L., (2009).Growing in Humility. C.S. Lewis Institute. https://www.cslewisinstitute.org/

> *"Humility is nothing more than the recognition of the truth about ourselves as fallen creatures; as redeemed creatures by God and acting consistently in that truth."* [78] (William L. Kynes, "Growing in Humility")

Indeed humility is a synonym for honesty[79]. It's the honest acknowledgment of our [spiritual] condition (self-condition), so we can genuinely cry to God for help. The *"Two Disciplines"* that Kynes shared on how we can grow in humility, balances the reality of our need and the greatness of God, as the ultimate source or reference for humility.

Two Disciplines to Grow in Humility[80]

---

[78] Kynes, W.L., (2009).*Growing in Humility*. C.S. Lewis Institute. https://www.cslewisinstitute.org/

[79]. Root, J., (2014).*Series: Growing in Humility* (Part 1). C.S. Lewis Institute. https://www.cslewisinstitute.org/

[80]. Kynes, W.L., (2009).Growing in Humility. C.S. Lewis Institute. https://www.cslewisinstitute.org/

Discipline in Truth	Discipline in Action
• *Grow in humility by reflecting upon the greatness of God (we are nothing before His greatness)* • *Grow in humility by reflecting upon the holiness of God (we are humble before God because we're sinners and forgiven)* • *Grow in humility by reflecting the grace of God (pride brings fear, while grace brings humbling hope)* • *Grow in humility by reflecting on His humility (Jesus' selflessness)*	*Must be done discretely and not attention seeker* • *Watch how you respond to the accusations or criticism from others (a humble person receives criticism readily)* • *Watch out how you respond in the pride of others (the pride of others offends you)* • *Watch out how you respond to hardships and slights (humility doesn't return evil for evil)* • *Watch who you associate with (no name-dropping deliberately perform some tasks that are "beneath your dignity"* • *If you find yourself delighting in someone*

	else's faults and failures, spend time thinking about your sins and imperfections. • Do some anonymous good deeds in the name of Christ (keep it anonymous) • Scrupulously avoid putting on a false front • Restrain from the urge to always give advice or offer your opinion (make it a practice to turn the conversation away from yourself) • Cultivate a heart of thanksgiving • Practice submission (learn to obey) • Give honor to others (rather than tearing them down; don't be envious of the success of others) • Do not fear in humility.

Looking at the *"Discipline in Action"* that Kynes shared, we're viewing a long journey for growth. We're guilty of not displaying or falling short in each action and have such a strong conviction to check ourselves if we truly understand Christlikeness. Because those actions are reflections of

Christ in ourselves - how we seek the power of the Holy Spirit and give serious attention to the modeling of Jesus Christ. Just like what Apostle Paul was saying to encourage the church in Philippians 2. His encouragement to follow Christ's modeling by doing Philippians 2:3-8; *(1) lowliness of mind (Philippians 2:3), (2) charitable attitude for the good of others exemplified in the life and death of Christ (Philippians 2:4-8).* But if we're not truly anchored in the Gospel, these acts could fall in "false modesty," or may stand as our "good works." That's why we need to constantly check or remind ourselves, *"Do we truly exemplify the life and death of Jesus Christ because we're faithfully experiencing the message of the Gospel?"*

> *"³Do nothing from selfishness or empty conceit, but with humility of mind regard one another as more important than yourselves; 4do not merely look out for your own personal interests, but also for the interests of others. 5Have this attitude in yourselves which was also in Christ Jesus, 6who, although He existed in the form of God, did not regard equality with God a thing to be grasped, 7but emptied Himself, taking the form of a bond-servant, and being made in the likeness of men. 8Being found in appearance as a man, He humbled Himself by becoming obedient to the point of death, even death on a cross."*
> Philippians 2:3-8, NASB1995

Apostle Paul started Philippians 2 with the word "therefore," which implies that he is expanding the exhortation from the previous chapter - Philippians 1:27-30: to steadfastness and confidence under persecution.

> *"²⁷Only conduct yourselves in a manner worthy of the gospel of Christ, so that whether I come and see you or remain*

absent, I will hear of you that you are standing firm in one spirit, with one mind striving together for the faith of the gospel; 28in no way alarmed by your opponents—which is a sign of destruction for them, but of salvation for you, and that too, from God. 29For to you it has been granted for Christ's sake, not only to believe in Him, but also to suffer for His sake, 30experiencing the same conflict which you saw in me, and now hear to be in me." (Philippians 1:27-30, NASB1995)

Don't be discouraged because we're seeing ourselves far from God's standard or be deceived by Satan to let this fear be taken out of context because we're seeing the reality of suffering in pursuing Christ. Rather have that conviction as the driving wheel to learn more about God, understand our connection with Him, and be dependent on Him. Let's not continue the journey of this life by soft-pedaling the message of the gospel (and discipleship) or even let ourselves move forward with a wrong understanding of God's standard of humility. In this lifetime journey of Christianity, humility is our greatest friend. This humility doesn't happen overnight. It's making daily choices of being intimate with God - hunger in His words, and opening our hearts for the influence of the Holy Spirit.

"Humility is not a grace that can be acquired in a few months; it is the work of a lifetime." (Francois Fenelon)[81]

---

[81] Tarrants, T. III (2011).Knowing & Doing: Pride and Humility. C.S. Lewis Institute. https://www.cslewisinstitute.org/

Apostle Paul continued in Philippians 2 that God's standard of humility glorifies Jesus Christ (Philippians 2:9), as well as leading each of us on our knees and confessing that Christ is our Lord (Philippians 2:10-11). Even when we're alone, we're working out our Salvation with "fear and trembling" (Philippians 2:12). This is not servile fear and slavish despondency that arise from doubt, but serious and filial fear implying deep humility and submissiveness of mind in reverence to the divine God[82]. Genuine humility starts with submission to Jesus Christ because He is the only One who can truly save us, and then it continues to this life journey under His lordship. Humility is the resulting actions from our relationship with Christ Jesus. So in application to our lives or in the context of any relationship particularly in marriage, it's taking bold changes to obey and follow God's will, and design for us, as well as the roles that He entrusted to us.

Rejoice

We can rejoice because Jesus Christ didn't just die on the cross to save us. He assures us that we'll have sufficient help in following Him through this life (particularly in humble submission to His lordship) - by the pouring out of the Holy Spirit.

[12]*"I have many more things to say to you, but you cannot bear them now.* [13]*But when He, the Spirit of truth, comes, He will guide you into all the truth; for He will not speak on His own initiative, but whatever He hears, He will speak; and He will disclose to you what is to come.* [14]*He will glorify Me, for He will take of Mine and will disclose it to you.* [15]*All things that the Father has are Mine; therefore I said that He takes of Mine and will disclose it to you."*
(John 16:12-15, NASB1995)

The Holy Spirit is there to be our guide (see also Romans 8:14). It is not only to show us the way but to go along with us for continued guidance and influence. The indwelling of the Holy Spirit defines our relationship with Christ while the continual infilling is the Holy Spirit's control over our lives. The Holy Spirit's guidance and influence is not just in the head of knowledge but the powerful change in our hearts leading us to progressive discovery of the truth. The Holy Spirit will complete the teachings of Jesus Christ. This undertaking is to glorify Jesus Christ! And we all may know how this story ends.

> *"These things I have spoken to you, so that in Me you may have peace. In the world you have tribulation, but take courage; I have overcome the world."* (John 16:33, NASB1995)

In whatever trouble we might be or our marriages might be in, Jesus' promise of peace should give us confidence and courage, because He overcame the world! He conquered it for us. He conquered it for our marriages. So, let's keep journeying with Jesus Christ - restore, relearn, and rejoice!

REY ABARCA & ANNIE ABARCA

Since 2019, they have been boldly sharing the gospel and discipleship through social media and during any organized gatherings. Their journey has fueled a passion for sharing God's transformative power in damaged and broken marriages like theirs. As a result, they created a non-profit organization called CJ2, Couples Journey in Christ Jesus.

Rey Abarca was only 12 years old when he moved to the USA from the Philippines. Despite facing challenges from a broken family, he found stability by joining the US Navy, where he completed 20 years of service. His desire to have his own family wasn't realized until after two broken marriages. Then he married Annie and had three children. He had initially planned to become a police officer after completing his studies in Criminal Justice. However, life circumstances led him to join Annie in business, and he equipped himself with several units in a Master's in Business Administration.

Annie Abarca paused her pursuit of a career in Chemical Engineering when she moved to the USA in 2007. Since then, she has become a stay-at-home mother. While pregnant with their third child, she pursued her Master's in Business Administration. After completing her degree, she created a business from her paper crafting hobby. Together with Rey, they were recognized as the SBA 2018 Minority-Owned Small Business of the Year for Nevada. Little did they know that this achievement would mark the turning point in a journey that was far from what they initially desired.

THANKS

Having the opportunity to review certain journeys in this life and share them through a book is not something we previously considered. Yet the overwhelming grace, mercy, and love of our amazing God cannot simply be sealed and kept. It needs to be told and shared because it's part of recognizing and giving back all the praise and glory to God. Despite this, we still face challenges in telling our stories, so it's only by His grace that we have the courage to obey and do so. Our journey from receiving the conviction to write this book, to finalizing its outline and completing every chapter, would not have been possible apart from God's help. This process has been beyond our comfort zone, and every page we accomplished started with prayer and a reliance on His promises. It wasn't until God changed our hearts that we found ourselves inclined to His words because reading had not been an enjoyable habit for us, much less writing and creating a book. In this moment of giving back praise and glory to Him, we truly mean it. To this day, we are still in awe of how this book has come to life.

The overflowing faithfulness of God didn't just see us through every bump in completing this book but also provided every resource that He orchestrated and directed. In addition to the authors, ministries, speakers, and even a movie mentioned in the footnotes, we would like to dedicate these last pages to recognizing certain organizations that have been impactful in our journey. First is the Christ Commission Fellowship, where we initially encountered and experienced discipleship. God used this church and the many people we've met through this movement to deepen our relationship with Him through discipleship. Second is the C.S. Lewis Institute, which generously offers a vast compilation of resources readily available for anyone seeking to learn more about God and this faith journey. C.S. Lewis's book, "The Problem of Pain," greatly aided us in navigating the recent painful season we went through before hearing God's conviction to write this book. Third is the Focus on the Family ministry. Their efforts to share Biblical truths and practical applications are evident in every podcast episode. It's always a blessing to hear stories from podcast guests, and the ministry's commitment to providing accessible learning resources through podcasts has been very effective for us, who constantly search for and desire to remain focused on learning while attending to our daily activities. We lift up to God every individual behind these ministries, as well as the other resources that can be found in our footnotes. May God continue to sustain them in sharing His truths and pointing many to Christ.

We're also thankful for our children, who have prayed with us constantly and sometimes join the conversations as we reminisce about God's ongoing work in our lives. Although this book focuses on our marital relationship, having our children alongside us in this journey has elevated our relearning experiences.

Lastly, we are thankful to you for choosing this book and considering it during your reading time. As first-time authors, we value and appreciate every opportunity to share our testimonies through the medium of book writing. We pray that you will be encouraged and grow in curiosity about a life anchored in Christ. Should you wish to continue this journey with us, we invite you to stay connected with the Couples' Journey ministry at www.couplesjourney.org.

Thank you very much.

Let's keep journeying with Christ Jesus,
Rey & Annie